THE
everyday
BIBLE
MEMORY
devotional
FOR
WOMEN

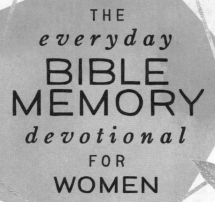

THE *everyday* BIBLE MEMORY *devotional* FOR WOMEN

365 DAYS IN GOD'S WORD

BARBOUR
PUBLISHING

HIDE GOD'S WORD IN YOUR HEART TODAY:
2 TIMOTHY 3:16-17

This scripture verse from 2 Timothy helps you remember just how important the Bible is in your daily routine: It provides truthful instruction, strengthens your faith, and prepares you to live a godly life.

The Everyday Bible Memory Devotional for Women is a plan to help you grow closer to your heavenly Father through insightful devotional thoughts, prayers, and scriptures. As you spend time each day with the Lord, you will find yourself more prepared for whatever life brings. Meditate on the thoughts, say the prayers, and memorize each daily scripture. Carry the scripture verses with you. Repeat them until the words come easily. Then apply them to your daily life. Take note of how applying the verses transforms you, your relationships with others, and most importantly your relationship with God.

Allow God's Word to bless you as it becomes a part of who you are.

Be blessed, and be a blessing to others by sharing His Word.

DAY 1

Memory Verse of the Day

"Be strong and of good courage; do not be afraid, nor be dismayed, for the LORD your God is with you wherever you go."

JOSHUA 1:9 NKJV

I AM STRONG.

God gives you strength and courage to face anything and everything. With Him, you can boldly go where no woman has gone before! Whenever fear creeps into your mind, say today's verse aloud and watch your doubts crumble before the presence of God!

Thank You, Lord, for Your strength and encouragement. With You at my side, I will not be afraid.

DAY 2

Memory Verse of the Day

Now all glory to God, who is able, through his mighty power at work within us, to accomplish infinitely more than we might ask or think.

EPHESIANS 3:20 NLT

I AM READY.

The things you can do when God is working through you are beyond your imagination, so don't limit yourself. Tap in to His infinite power, connect to His Spirit, and let Him take the reins on your life. The results will be awesome!

God, I stand at the ready. Work through me!

DAY 3

Memory Verse of the Day

"And when you pray, do not use meaningless repetition as the Gentiles do, for they think they will be heard because of their many words."

MATTHEW 6:7 AMP

TEACH ME TO PRAY.

God does not judge your way with words. He knows your heart. He wants to hear from you. When you pray, first honor Him as Creator, Master, Savior, and Lord. Reflect on who He is and praise Him. Then confess and repent of your sins. Thank your heavenly Father, and make your requests known to Him.

Lord, Your Word says that my prayers rise up to heaven like incense from the earth. Remind me daily to send prayers Your way!

DAY 4

Memory Verse of the Day

I have composed and quieted my soul;
like a weaned child rests against his mother,
my soul is like a weaned child within me.

PSALM 131:2 NASB

QUIET MY SOUL.

Do you sometimes feel like escaping from the world's wild ride? When things of this world cannot satisfy you, remember that God can. Let Him wean you from your daily worries. Like a small child, crawl up onto your heavenly Father's lap. Breathe deeply. Relax in His presence and allow your soul to find rest.

Father God, take me in Your arms.
Hold me tight. Fill me with Your comforting peace.

DAY 5

Memory Verse of the Day

*To everything there is a season,
a time for every purpose under heaven.*

ECCLESIASTES 3:1 NKJV

CHANGE HAPPENS.

There are seasons when everything falls into place and seasons when nothing appears to go right. Seasons change. But, with each change God gives you a fresh opportunity to recapture your hopes and dreams. You need only to open your heart, step out in faith, and trust Him.

*Dear God, when things change,
for better or worse, remind me to have
faith and put all of my trust in You.*

DAY 6

Memory Verse of the Day

For as he thinks within himself, so he is.

PROVERBS 23:7 NASB

WHO CARES WHAT *THEY* THINK!

Don't worry about what others think about you. Live your life to please God alone. He knows your heart. When you allow yourself to be real before Him, it doesn't matter what others think. If the God of the universe has accepted you, then who cares about someone else's opinion?

Dear Lord, may I live for You alone. Help me transition from a people pleaser to a God pleaser.

DAY 7

Memory Verse of the Day

The LORD is close to all who call on him, yes, to all who call on him in truth.

PSALM 145:18 NLT

GOD IS ALWAYS NEAR.

God's truth anchors your faith, and your faith gets His attention. God wants you to know He is nearby. He waits for you to grasp all that He has for you and to reap the blessings that come your way when you enter into a trusting relationship with Him.

Dear Lord, help me to believe and trust that You are always near me.

DAY 8

Memory Verse of the Day

A joyful heart is good medicine,
but a broken spirit dries up the bones.

PROVERBS 17:22 NASB

OH, HAPPY DAY!

Did you feel like crawling back into bed this morning? Wake up! God has something wonderful waiting for you. Joy. It works like medicine but has no negative side effects. Today, raise your hands to the sky, promise to be happy, and praise God for joy—even if you don't feel like it.

Father God, today help me to remember
that You are the Source of my joy.

DAY 9

"For I know the plans I have for you,"
declares the Lord, *"plans to prosper you*
and not to harm you, plans to give
you hope and a future."

JEREMIAH 29:11 NIV

GOD HAS A PLAN FOR ME.

Do you sometimes worry about finances and your future? Relax. God has a perfect plan for you. He has your life all worked out. Whew! Isn't that a relief? Unlike some of today's financial institutions, you can "bank" on God with absolute assurance. He promises you prosperity and fills your future with hope.

I'm not sure what the future holds, Lord,
but I trust Your plans and await Your blessings.

DAY 10

Memory Verse of the Day

For the LORD gives wisdom; from His mouth come knowledge and understanding. He stores up sound wisdom for the upright; He is a shield to those who walk in integrity, guarding the paths of justice, and He preserves the way of His godly ones.

PROVERBS 2:6–8 NASB

HELP ME GROW IN WISDOM.

God's Word says that wisdom comes from the mouth of God, from the very words He speaks. The Bible was written through the inspiration of the Holy Spirit. Know that if you hold fast to the precepts in God's Word, you will walk in integrity. Your feet will be planted on the straight and narrow road.

Lord, please give me the gift of Your guidance and help me to become wise through Your Word.

DAY 11

Memory Verse of the Day

"You did not choose me, but I chose you and appointed you that you should go and bear fruit and that your fruit should abide, so that whatever you ask the Father in my name, he may give it to you."

JOHN 15:16 ESV

YOU CHOSE ME?!

The Lord of all creation chose YOU! He saw you in your sinful state and said, "I'll take that one. I will adopt her and make her My own." Now He longs for you to "bear fruit"—to lead by His example—so that you can guide others toward Him.

Father God, thank You for choosing me to be Your own. Help me today to lead others to You.

DAY 12

Memory Verse of the Day

Thank you for making me so wonderfully complex!
Your workmanship is marvelous—how well I know it.

I AM PERFECTLY ME!

God thinks you are perfect just the way you are. He adores you, and He wants you to know just how much. On days when you're feeling down and need a boost of assurance, remember not only who you are—but *whose* you are. You belong to the King!

Father God, thank You for the fine
job You did in making me.

DAY 13

Memory Verse of the Day

*The heartfelt counsel of a friend
is as sweet as perfume and incense.*

PROVERBS 27:9 NLT

MY WORDS ARE IMPORTANT.

Words not only convey a message, they also reveal the attitude of your heart. Whether you are communicating with friends, family, or coworkers today, show that you value them. In all your conversations, extend God's grace to those hungry to experience His love. Be encouraging. Seek to build them up.

*Dear Lord, may I view each conversation as
an opportunity to extend Your grace to others.*

DAY 14

*"Incline your ear and come to Me.
Listen, that you may live."*

Isaiah 55:3 nasb

MMM. . .LIFESAVERS.

God's Word is filled with lifesavers—lifesaving scripture, that is. All you need to do is read His Word, listen for His message within the scriptures, and put His to-do plan into action. God's Word is sweeter than candy. And it's good to "eat" a little every day.

*I'm opening myself up to You and
Your Word, Lord. Show me how to live!*

DAY 15

Memory Verse of the Day

*I call to God; GOD will help me. At dusk, dawn,
and noon I sigh deep sighs—he hears, he rescues.*

PSALM 55:17 MSG

WAKE ME UP, JESUS!

Are you dragging this morning? Start your day with a
cup of tea or coffee, and Jesus. He is the best listener,
and He can transform a sour mood into a cheerful one.
A little time spent with Him can work wonders. Like no
one else, Jesus can turn morning into cause for rejoicing.

*Wake me up, Jesus! Light up my
day with sunshine and joy.*

DAY 16

Memory Verse of the Day

Sing to the LORD a new song;
Sing to the LORD, all the earth.

PSALM 96:1 NASB

I WILL SING TO THE LORD.

Start your day by singing to the Lord. Think about how rhythm is the heartbeat of a song. In giving us rhythm for our music and lives, our Creator has put His song in our hearts. May your song return to Him with a richness that brings honor to His glorious name.

Lord, I will sing to You a morning song
with words of honor and praise.

DAY 17

Memory Verse of the Day

In him we live, and move, and have our being.

ACTS 17:28 KJV

IT'S A NEW DAY.

It's a new day in which God has given you breath and life. Relish the days He gives you. Take the opportunities He affords you. Cherish the love He has bestowed upon you and share it with others. Get out there, enjoy, and live this day to the fullest.

Lord, thank You for the gift of life and breath!

DAY 18

Memory Verse of the Day

*"Don't you realize that I could ask my Father
for thousands of angels to protect us,
and he would send them instantly?"*

MATTHEW 26:53 NLT

LORD, PROTECT ME.

Whenever you need protection you can breathe a huge sigh of relief, because you have all the protection you need. God Himself protects you from anything evil. He intervenes, ready to take it on full-force. He is your defense. When you need help, speak His name: "Father God." He's there. Always.

*Thank You, Father, for being my
protection all the time, wherever I go.*

DAY 19

Memory Verse of the Day

*Be careful to obey all these regulations I
am giving you, so that it may always go well
with you and your children after you, because
you will be doing what is good and right
in the eyes of the LORD your God.*

DEUTERONOMY 12:28 NIV

GUIDE ME, LORD. TEACH ME.

When our children disobey, we feel disappointed and
maybe sense that they don't love us. We think that if
they did, they would understand that our instructions
are meant to guide them. This is how God feels when
you fail to obey Him. He connects love with obedience.
Do your best to obey Him today.

*God, today and every day, teach me and guide
my steps. Help me to obey You in all that I do.*

DAY 20

I pray that God, the source of hope, will fill you completely with joy and peace because you trust in him. Then you will overflow with confident hope through the power of the Holy Spirit.

ROMANS 15:13 NLT

IT'S ALL ABOUT FAITH.

God wants to fill you to the brim with joy and peace. But to receive joy and peace, you need to have faith in Him. Today, place your confidence in God, who, in His timing, will complete that task, mend that relationship, or do whatever else you need.

Help me to grow in faith, God,
knowing that You are the Source of my joy.

DAY 21

Memory Verse of the Day

*Indeed, nothing in all creation will ever be
able to separate us from the love of God.*

ROMANS 8:39 NLT

YOU LOVE ME.
YOU *REALLY* LOVE ME!

Some people shut God out because they feel ashamed
of their sins. But you know better. In those times you
need to cling to the assuring words in today's memory
verse and be confident in God's unfailing, unconditional
love. Nothing can separate you from His love—nothing.

*I will not shut You out, God, because I know that
You love me all the time, regardless of my sins.*

DAY 22

Memory Verse of the Day

*But more than anything else, put God's
work first and do what he wants. Then
the other things will be yours as well.*

MATTHEW 6:33 CEV

LORD, YOU'RE #1.

Your heavenly Father gives you opportunities to check
your priorities. He puts you in situations where you
have to choose between Him and your own desires.
Putting yourself first brings frustration. Your work produces little progress. But when you put Him first, especially when you don't want to, He blesses you with joy.

*Father, I often forget to make You my priority.
Help me today, and every day, to put You first.*

DAY 23

Memory Verse of the Day

Let the weak say, I am strong [a warrior]!
JOEL 3:10 AMPC

LOOK! I'M A WARRIOR!

As a child of God, you have amazing resources at your fingertips. One of those is His strength. You need not be a worrier when God has equipped you to be a warrior. Let "I am strong" be your battle cry today, then watch God help you to smash whatever gets in your way!

You are my Stronghold, Lord! Victory is ours!

DAY 24

Memory Verse of the Day

*Every good and perfect gift is from above,
coming down from the Father of the heavenly lights,
who does not change like shifting shadows.*

James 1:17 niv

I WILL WATCH FOR BLESSINGS. . .

It's up to you to recognize the opportunities God has for you. Watch for His blessings. Listen to His direction and instruction so you can be quick to notice every good and perfect gift. God wants you to experience His favors and blessings, so expect Him to meet you at every turn.

*Lord, thank You for setting favor and
blessing in my path and help me to expect
it wherever I go, whatever I do.*

DAY 25

Memory Verse of the Day

"I love those who love me,
and those who seek me find me."

PROVERBS 8:17 NCV

WHERE ARE YOU, GOD?

When you seek God, you expect to find Him, but sometimes it's as if He's hiding. He might be holding back waiting for a change in your heart, or He's speaking in a still, small voice, wanting you to be quiet and hear Him. Keep seeking. He's right there, waiting for you to find Him.

Dear God, I'm listening. What do You need from me? I want to feel close to You again.

DAY 26

Memory Verse of the Day

*My confusion is continually before me,
and the shame of my face hath covered me.*

PSALM 44:15 KJV

CLUTTER, BE GONE!

The burdening clutter of negative thinking and bad choices keeps you from accomplishing what God wants you to do. Gather your clutter, relinquish it to Him, and allow Him to remove the burden from you. If spiritual clutter starts piling up again, remember—you can repeat the process every day.

*Heavenly Father, I don't want all this clutter
in my life. Take it. It's Yours. Help me
to keep it from piling up again.*

DAY 27

Memory Verse of the Day

*Those who say they live in God
should live their lives as Jesus did.*

1 John 2:6 nlt

I WILL BE LIKE JESUS.

Much is said about superheroes these days, but the
only true "superhero" is Jesus Christ, who will never
fail you. He alone was fully God and fully man. He alone
possesses perfectly all the characteristics we most
admire. Read about Him in God's Word and strive to
be like Him.

*Jesus, I want to be more like You. Teach me
through the Bible how to live a life like Yours.*

DAY 28

Memory Verse of the Day

*I have learned how to be content
with whatever I have.*

Philippians 4:11 nlt

PLEASE, GIVE ME WHAT I NEED.

There's no good purpose in wishing for what you don't
have. Instead, find delight in what you *do* have! God
promises to provide for you. Tell Him what you want
when you pray, and trust Him to provide exactly what
you need. He will not let you down.

*As my Father, Lord, You have supplied me
with all I need. Thank You—for everything!*

DAY 29

Memory Verse of the Day

*Beloved, do not imitate what is evil, but what
is good. The one who does good is of God;
the one who does evil has not seen God.*

3 John 1:11 nasb

I WANT TO BE LIKE YOU.

As a child of God, His character is yours to imitate. The
enemy entices you toward an "everyone does it" mindset. But as you immerse yourself in God's Word, you
grow in knowledge through His sound teaching. When
you apply the truth of His Word, you become more
like Him.

*Lord, teach me through Your scriptures
and help me to apply them to my life.*

DAY 30

Memory Verse of the Day

God has given each of you a gift from
his great variety of spiritual gifts.

1 PETER 4:10 NLT

I AM *SO* TALENTED!

God has given you special gifts—things that you are good at—designed to be a blessing to others. Think about your God-given talents. Breathe new life into them. Allow them to shine, reflecting the love and glory of God. Use them to bless others—that's why God gave them to you.

Dear God, remind me of my God-given talents.
Help me to use them today to bless others.

DAY 31

Memory Verse of the Day

Make this your common practice:
Confess your sins to each other and
pray for each other so that you can
live together whole and healed.

JAMES 5:16 MSG

THIS IS THE *REAL* ME.

Too often, we miss the value of sharing our failings.
When you share your own experiences—especially your
failures—you gain empathy, you're more approachable,
and you increase your "relatability" to others. Let your
guard down today and be who you are. Be the real
you—flawed maybe, but someone striving to please God.

Lord, help me to be real with those You have put
around me. I pray that they see You through
me and it draws them closer to You.

DAY 32

Our LORD and our God, you are like the sun and also like a shield. You treat us with kindness and with honor, never denying any good thing to those who live right.

PSALM 84:11 CEV

FORGIVE ME. BLESS ME.

Aren't you glad that God doesn't stop the flow of blessings in your life when you mess up? He bestows kindness and honor and doesn't withhold from those who try to live right. Sure, you're not perfect, but as long as you ask for forgiveness for your mess-ups, God's right there, ready to bless you.

Thank You, God, for blessing me with honor and kindness, even when I don't deserve it.

DAY 33

Memory Verse of the Day

*I focus on this one thing: Forgetting the past
and looking forward to what lies ahead.*

PHILIPPIANS 3:13 NLT

TODAY, I AM WHERE I SHOULD BE.

Wherever God has placed you today is exactly where
you should be. Your job is to find out what you can do
there to accomplish His purpose. Forget what happened
yesterday. Focus instead on God. Ask Him to guide you,
then watch His miracles unfold!

*I thank You for where I am today, Lord.
Show me what to do!*

DAY. 34

Memory Verse of the Day

And He said to them, "Come away by yourselves to a secluded place and rest a while." (For there were many people coming and going, and they did not even have time to eat.)

MARK 6:31 NASB

THERE'S BEAUTY ALL AROUND.

Take time today to stop and notice God's artistry: majestic mountains, plum and brown with snowy white tops; streaks of red, yellow, and violet spread like fingers in a sunrise or sunset; the deep blue ocean and the turquoise sea. God made all creation—then He rested and admired His work.

*God, Your works are magnificent! Thank You—
not only for them, but also for reminding
me to stop and take notice.*

DAY 35

Memory Verse of the Day

*"Therefore everyone who confesses
Me before men, I will also confess him
before My Father who is in heaven."*

MATTHEW 10:32 NASB

JESUS IS MINE!

Jesus came to earth as God in the flesh. God had tried to save us from sin by giving us His laws. He sent us His prophets, but people refused to listen. Finally, He sent His Son, Jesus, to save us so we can have eternal life in heaven. Oh, what a Savior we have in Him!

*God, how good of You to love me so much that
You sent me a Savior. Hallelujah! Jesus is mine!*

DAY 36

Taste and see that the LORD is good.
Oh, the joys of those who take refuge in him!
PSALM 34:8 NLT

I NEED COFFEE!

Are you a morning-coffee person? There's something about the smell of coffee brewing and that first taste that wakes you up and makes you ready for the day. Meet Jesus for coffee this morning. Talk with Him. Take pleasure in Him. Taste and see that the Lord is good!

Lord Jesus, come. Talk with me. Provide me
with all that I need to enter this day joyfully.

DAY 37

Memory Verse of the Day

*And my God will meet all your needs according
to the riches of his glory in Christ Jesus.*

PHILIPPIANS 4:19 NIV

GOD GIVES ME WHAT I NEED.

Aren't you glad that God is your ultimate Supplier?
When you're feeling depleted and when you don't think
there's anything inside of you left to give, He supplies
you with strength, courage, tenacity, and favor. He won't
fail you. God will always come through as your Supplier.
That's a promise you can trust.

*Dear God, thank You for meeting my
needs with Your endless supply of mercy.*

DAY 38

Memory Verse of the Day

"I will ask the Father, and he will give you another
Counselor to be with you forever—the Spirit of truth."
JOHN 14:16–17 NIV 1984

THE HOLY SPIRIT IS MY HELPER.

We were not created to be alone. God made us social
beings, dependent on one another, dependent on Him.
Jesus sent the Holy Spirit to be your Helper. Ask and
you can experience His comfort, counsel, and guidance
immediately—right now. He is closer than you can ever
imagine.

*Dear Jesus, send the Holy Spirit to guide me today.
Remind me throughout the day that my Helper is near.*

DAY 39

Memory Verse of the Day

Because of Christ and our faith in him, we can now come boldly and confidently into God's presence.

EPHESIANS 3:12 NLT

LORD, GIVE ME CONFIDENCE.

Jesus walked in total God-confidence—knowing that His steps were planned. He had only to listen to His Father's heartbeat to know which way to go. Today, try living in total God-confidence, knowing that you'll be able to withstand anything life throws at you, because God is with you.

Father, please give me all the confidence I need today to overcome any obstacle in my path.

DAY 40

Memory Verse of the Day

But those who hope in the Lord will renew their strength. They will soar on wings like eagles; they will run and not grow weary, they will walk and not be faint.

Isaiah 40:31 niv

GOD HOLDS MY HAND.

Life can sometimes feel like you're at the edge of a cliff and about to fall off. Remember—God is the only constant, the only One who without a doubt can shield you from trouble. He will always lift you up. Put your hand in His, and you won't fall.

Lord, You are my safe haven. As I abide in You today, fill me with Your strength.

DAY 41

Memory Verse of the Day

*The Lord GOD is my strength, and He
has made my feet like hinds' feet,
and makes me walk on my high places.*

HABAKKUK 3:19 NASB

WHAT IF I STUMBLE?

Your heavenly Father frees you from dread of danger as
you scale the rugged terrain of your life. You can hike
a trail of uncertainty with confidence, knowing God is
with you. If you stumble, in His mercy He will pick you
up, strengthen you, and set you back on your feet.

*Lord, as long as I hold tight to Your hand, I know that I
won't stumble through life. I will put my trust in You.*

DAY 42

Memory Verse of the Day

Do not merely listen to the word, and so deceive yourselves. Do what it says.

JAMES 1:22 NIV

I WILL LIVE GOD'S WORD.

We're promised in the Word of God that we are capable of sticking with it. We can read the Word of God, absorb the Word of God, and live the Word of God. It's doable. And this heavenly "sticktoitiveness" means we can see each project—and each challenge—from start to finish.

Heavenly Father, the Bible has all that I need to meet any challenge. Help me to absorb Your Word and to live by it.

DAY 43

Memory Verse of the Day

*"Then young women will dance and be glad,
young men and old as well. I will turn their
mourning into gladness; I will give them
comfort and joy instead of sorrow."*

JEREMIAH 31:13 NIV

GOD TURNS SAD HEARTS GLAD.

Don't you love this promise in today's scripture verse?
God can turn a sad heart glad! This joy comes as a free
gift. You don't have to earn it. You don't have to beg
for it. Just reach out and grab it, then watch as you are
strengthened for the days ahead.

Thank You, God, for the promise of gladness.

DAY 44

Memory Verse of the Day

My soul, wait thou only upon God;
for my expectation is from him.

PSALM 62:5 KJV

I CAN EXPECT GOOD THINGS.

The one thing you can count on is God. Simply have patience, confident He will do as promised. Go out today with assurance, expecting good things from the Lord; in doing so, you'll find that your cup runneth over!

I wait upon You only, God.
My hands are open, waiting to receive!

DAY 45

Memory Verse of the Day

*You died to this life, and your real
life is hidden with Christ in God.*

COLOSSIANS 3:3 NLT

WHAT IF I ONLY SEE SCARS?

You may wish that you could hide the scars in the picture of your life. But those impressions have meaning
and purpose; everything you see as a scar is evidence
of a wound that God has healed. When you look at
your life, you only see the blemishes. But God sees
your beauty.

*My loving Father, thank You for seeing
the beauty in me. Help me to see it too.*

DAY 46

Memory Verse of the Day

*Let no corrupt communication proceed out of your
mouth, but that which is good to the use of edifying,
that it may minister grace unto the hearers.*

EPHESIANS 4:29 KJV

MY WORDS WILL HONOR GOD. . .

Imagine if a filter were placed over your mouth to cap-
ture all your distasteful words. How dirty would that
filter become? God wants your words to be soothing
and inspiring, never bitter or distasteful. Ask Him to
help with your words today. Use them to bring God's
message of love to those around you.

*Heavenly Father, forgive my harsh and
bitter words. Help me to filter my speech
so I may bring comfort and joy to others.*

DAY 47

Memory Verse of the Day

The LORD is King forever and ever;
nations have perished from His land.

PSALM 10:16 NASB

JESUS IS KING—NOW AND FOREVER!

Satan devotes all his efforts to eradicating Christianity. His influence is ugly, but it will not be permanent. The reason? God's Son, Jesus, lives forever within those who call upon His name. He is and will remain King and will one day come back to claim this earth for His own, forever and ever.

Lord, as this world becomes increasingly evil,
remind me that You're coming back to
claim all that is rightfully Yours.

DAY 48

Memory Verse of the Day

*I will instruct you and teach you
in the way you should go.*

Psalm 32:8 niv

HE SHOWS ME THE WAY.

God knows which way you should go. You need to play your part of course, seeking His guidance, listening for it, and then following it. Knowing that it is God who has pointed you in a certain direction can give you peace of mind and confidence in the decisions you make.

*Father, show me the way. Teach me to seek Your
guidance and to make the right decisions.*

DAY 49

Memory Verse of the Day

Whoever gives heed to instruction prospers,
*and blessed is the one who trusts in the L*ORD.

PROVERBS 16:20 NIV

IF I READ THE INSTRUCTIONS. . .

Do you read directions, or do you jump right in and try to do it all on your own? Sometimes, only when we fail, do we read the instructions. Before walking out the door this morning, find inspiration and instruction from scripture. Then trust in God's guidance, and you will prosper as promised!

Thank You, Lord, for Your Guidebook
and for helping me to walk Your way.

DAY 50

Memory Verse of the Day

*Be joyful in hope, patient in affliction,
faithful in prayer.*

ROMANS 12:12 NIV

I NEED A BOOST!

Sometimes, even a sunny morning isn't enough to send you joyfully into the day. Solar energy is the new green. But it's got nothing on God, the mightiest power source you have. Need recharging? Put your hope in God. Plug in to His promises. He'll give you strength to get through the day.

*Lord, I need a boost of energy. Fill me with
Your power so that I can have a productive day.*

DAY 51

Memory Verse of the Day

Satisfy us in the morning with your unfailing love,
that we may sing for joy and be glad all our days.
PSALM 90:14 NIV

I AM SATISFIED.

What joy, to live a satisfied life. No cravings. No longings. No "what-ifs." Just a blissful state of realizing that all you could ever want is right in front of you. And it is, you know, because God is right there, totally in control, meeting your every need.

Heavenly Father, You satisfy all my needs,
every day, all day. Thank You!

DAY 52

Memory Verse of the Day

Two people are better off than one,
for they can help each other succeed.

ECCLESIASTES 4:9 NLT

FRIENDS AT WORK. . .

Solitary work is sometimes necessary, but too much solitude can lead to sluggishness and dull ideas. God provides us with friends at work to help us not only get the job done, but also to succeed. Seek out God-loving friends at work. Team up with them and rely on each other for help.

Lord, lead me to friends at work who love
You as I do. Two, or more, are better than one!

DAY 53

Memory Verse of the Day

*" Truly I tell you, if anyone says to this
mountain, 'Go, throw yourself into the sea,'
and does not doubt in their heart but believes that
what they say will happen, it will be done for them."*

MARK 11:23 NIV

MY FAITH CAN MOVE MOUNTAINS.

When faced with an obstacle that won't budge, put
on your faith glasses and see it through God's eyes.
Then, with all of the confidence you can muster, holler
to that mountain, "Hey you! Get out of here!" Might
sound childish, but that kind of faith could just clear
the road in front of you!

*Lord, by putting my faith in You, nothing will get in my
way. I have faith, Lord—but please, give me more.*

DAY 54

Memory Verse of the Day

Do not neglect to show hospitality to strangers, for by this some have entertained angels without knowing it.

Hebrews 13:2 nasb

I MIGHT MEET AN ANGEL.

God calls us to help in precarious situations. When you help a stranger, or let one assist you, you won't know if the stranger is an angel, or if the presumed angel is a mere human—but God knows. Listen to your heart and be watchful. God might ask you to help a stranger today.

Dear God, today I will watch for someone in need and listen for Your guidance. Show me how I can help.

DAY 55

Memory Verse of the Day

*"Blessed are those who mourn,
for they shall be comforted."*

Matthew 5:4 nasb

I WILL MEET SADNESS HEAD-ON.

No one escapes sadness. God knows that grieving alone can deepen the sorrow, so He puts friends and family members in people's lives to comfort them. It is His blessing. You can show the love of Christ when you sit with grieving friends and let them talk, or let them cry, or cry with them.

*Lord, sometimes I shy away from sadness.
Teach me to be a comfort to those who
are mourning. Show me how I can help.*

DAY 56

Memory Verse of the Day

The LORD came and stood there, calling as at the other times, "Samuel! Samuel!" Then Samuel said, "Speak, for your servant is listening."

1 SAMUEL 3:10 NIV

SPEAK, LORD. I'M LISTENING.

God speaks powerfully through His Word, the Bible, and also whispers truth to our hearts. He most often communicates to servant hearts that are ready to listen—hearts committed to obedience. Is your heart receptive to His call today? Work toward being able to say sincerely, "Speak, Lord, Your servant is listening!"

Dear Lord, bless me with a servant's heart, a heart committed to obedience.

DAY 57

Memory Verse of the Day

God decided in advance to adopt us into his own family by bringing us to himself through Jesus Christ. This is what he wanted to do, and it gave him great pleasure.

EPHESIANS 1:5 NLT

I AM GOD'S CHILD.

That day when God ushered you into His family, all of the promises in His Word became yours. God received great pleasure from adopting you as His own. What joy to be included in His eternal family! You can't help but celebrate that your heavenly Father chose you.

Heavenly Father, thank You for choosing me to be Your child. Knowing that I am Yours fills my heart with joy.

DAY 58

Memory Verse of the Day

"Ask, and it will be given to you; seek, and you will find; knock, and it will be opened to you."

MATTHEW 7:7 NASB

COME ON IN.

Are you looking for direction? Do you need help with a problem? God's door is always open. He'll give you the answers, help you find what you're looking for, and provide you with opportunities when you knock. Don't just sit there! Come on in. The Lord is waiting for you.

Father God, here I am—asking, seeking, knocking.

DAY 59

Memory Verse of the Day

*"I know that you can do all things;
no plan of yours can be thwarted."*

JOB 42:2 NIV 1984

BUT, WHY?

Sometimes what you think should happen, doesn't. But rest assured, God has a great plan for your life. All you need to do is be patient and let Him work it out. He can turn ashes into beauty. What a wonderful God you have! Expect good things from Him today.

*I have so many "whys," Lord, but I
believe that You will somehow work
everything out for my good. Thank You.*

DAY 60

Memory Verse of the Day

Be strong in the Lord and in his mighty power.

EPHESIANS 6:10 NIV

GOD IS MY POWER SOURCE.

Meditate on this today: God is like the wind, a powerful, unseen force that lifts you above your circumstances and enables you to dance amid your difficulties. He is the power and energy that gives you strength to carry on, in every way, despite any opposing force that tempts you to quit.

Lord, like leaves on the wind, lift me up
and let me dance above the storm.

DAY 61

Memory Verse of the Day

*The LORD is good, a strong
refuge when trouble comes.*

NAHUM 1:7 NLT

I NEED THE RAIN.

When rain falls on your life, you might not always experience it as something refreshing. But there is good reason to rejoice in the rain. Why? Because the seeds God planted in you, possibly many seasons earlier, need gentle rain for steady growth—and occasional storms for strengthening growth.

*Father, when rain comes into my life,
remind me to rejoice, knowing that
You are working to strengthen me.*

DAY 62

Memory Verse of the Day

*The fear of the LORD prolongs life, but the
years of the wicked will be shortened.*

PROVERBS 10:27 NASB

I WILL LEAD MY CHILDREN TO YOU.

Instead of being a cause of terror in your heart, the
phrase "fear of the Lord" means to reverence and honor
Him as your God. He alone is God, righteous and wise
enough to intervene and effect positive changes in your
life. Instilling this truth in your children enables them
to know His ways.

*God, I will teach my children to honor You.
I will instruct them in Your ways.*

DAY 63

Memory Verse of the Day

God is faithful, who has called you into
fellowship with his Son, Jesus Christ our Lord.

1 CORINTHIANS 1:9 NIV

JESUS IS MY COMPANION.

Today's scripture holds an amazing promise: God has called you to fellowship (to have companionship) with His Son, Jesus. Your Savior is with you, ready to dry your tears and give you strength and courage to put one foot in front of the other. Jesus is your Companion. Wow! What a blessed privilege.

Jesus, how wonderful that You are my constant Companion! I love it that You are my dearest Friend.

DAY 64

Memory Verse of the Day

*"You are the salt of the earth. But if the salt loses
its saltiness, how can it be made salty again?
It is no longer good for anything, except to be
thrown out and trampled underfoot."*

MATTHEW 5:13 NIV

I CAN LIVE A SALTY LIFE!

What a wonderful promise from God, that you can be
"salt" for those whose lives are bland without Him. Your
daily routine might seem mundane to you, but others
are watching and learning from your dedication to the
Lord, family, and friends. Their lives are being flavored
by your faithfulness.

*Dear God, help me always to present a good
example of what it means to lead a godly life.*

DAY 65

*We know that in all things God works
for the good of those who love him.*

Romans 8:28 niv

I'M ABOUT TO BOIL OVER!

Sometimes, in the heat of things, your angry emotions
might spill over. You won't make a good impression if
that happens. God knows when you're near your boil-
ing point, and He is there to help. When anger rises up
inside you, focus on Him, and He will keep you in check.

*Father God, when anger overwhelms me,
remind me to stop and allow You
to control my emotions.*

DAY 66

Memory Verse of the Day

*In the day of trouble he will keep
me safe in his dwelling.*

PSALM 27:5 NIV

DANGER! DANGER!

There are many dangers in this world, and you cannot escape them unless you are in God's safe house. Where He dwells, nothing can ever truly harm you. When you run to Him, He opens the door to you, spreading His protective arms to cover you. God is always there, waiting.

*Heavenly Father, when storms rage I find
comfort in knowing there is a safe haven ahead.*

DAY 67

Memory Verse of the Day

*No, dear brothers and sisters, I have not achieved it,
but I focus on this one thing: Forgetting the past
and looking forward to what lies ahead.*

PHILIPPIANS 3:13 NLT

FORWARD, MARCH. . .

Try walking forward while looking behind you. You
can't do it without stumbling, right? Now walk facing
forward and pay attention to what's around you. A
new opportunity lies ahead. So, instead of lamenting
past decisions, hurts, and failures, move forward knowing that God is leading you to greater opportunities.

*Lord, help me move forward, knowing You are with
me every step of the way. Better days await me!*

DAY 68

Memory Verse of the Day

Let us test and examine our ways,
and return to the LORD!

LAMENTATIONS 3:40 ESV

I WILL EXAMINE MY WAYS.

Take time today to examine your lifestyle. Is it pleasing to the Lord, or does it separate you from Him? The Holy Spirit will gently show you your sins, if you ask. Confess them to God so you may experience His forgiveness and your fellowship with Him can be restored.

God, help me to be willing to examine my
ways. Speak to me, through Your Holy Spirit,
of what is wrong in my life.

DAY 69

Memory Verse of the Day

How can a young person stay on the path of purity?
By living according to your word.

PSALM 119:9 NIV

GOD'S WORD IN THE MORNING. . .

The Bible contains true stories of kingdoms, journeys, wars, and love—sixty-six small books, all of them tied together. It begins with the creation of a perfect world, follows the world through its downfall, and ends victoriously with everything restored. Start each day with God's Word. Allow its truths to lead you.

Lord, lead me into the day with Your Word.
Keep it in my heart all day through.

DAY 70

Memory Verse of the Day

He saith unto them, Follow me,
and I will make you fishers of men.

MATTHEW 4:19 KJV

GO, FISH!

Jesus called Simon Peter and his brother, Andrew, into His ministry because they knew how to catch fish. Today, Jesus calls you to do just what Peter and Andrew did—cast your net with the love of Christ and draw in new believers for the kingdom of God. Make that your mission today.

Jesus, today I will make it a priority to tell others about You and invite them to enter God's kingdom.

DAY 71

Memory Verse of the Day

"Martha, Martha," the Lord answered,
"you are worried and upset about many things."

Luke 10:41 niv

MARTHA, MARTHA, MARTHA!

When Jesus visited His friends Mary and Martha, He reprimanded Martha for being too busy. Mary spent all her time with Jesus listening to His wisdom, but Martha was more concerned about being a good hostess and the preparations she had to make. Be like Mary today. Make Jesus your priority.

Jesus, forgive me for being too distracted
by worldly issues to spend time with You.
Here I am, Lord, ready to listen.

DAY 72

Memory Verse of the Day

For the word of God is alive and active. Sharper
than any double-edged sword, it penetrates even
to dividing soul and spirit, joints and marrow;
it judges the thoughts and attitudes of the heart.

HEBREWS 4:12 NIV

THERE IS POWER IN GOD'S WORD.

Have you memorized each day's scripture? If not, don't give up. Start again with today's verse. Each scripture you memorize is like a weapon against evil. When life turns you upside down, you can right yourself with God's Word. Whenever you apply it to your life, you release His mighty power.

Father, sometimes I get busy and forget to store
Your Word in my heart. I will try to do better.

DAY 73

Memory Verse of the Day

Know therefore that the LORD your God is God;
he is the faithful God, keeping his covenant of
love to a thousand generations of those who
love him and keep his commandments.

DEUTERONOMY 7:9 NIV

HE NEVER LETS ME DOWN.

God is always true to His word. If He says it, He will
do it. He won't ever let you down. Your Father agrees
never to leave or forsake you. Did you hear that? *Never!*
That's a promise you can genuinely trust. He says it and
He will do it.

Dear God, thank You for Your eternal faithfulness.
Thank You for never letting me down.

DAY 74

Memory Verse of the Day

A man who endures trials is blessed, because when he passes the test he will receive the crown of life that God has promised to those who love Him.

JAMES 1:12 HCSB

IF AT FIRST I DON'T SUCCEED. . .

How do you handle difficulties? Do the words "I'm not good enough" play through your head? God says that you *are* good enough. He gives you the power to endure your challenges and to keep on trying. A positive attitude plus endurance equals success. Remember that with every challenge you meet today.

Dear Lord, I will keep my eyes fixed on You and keep moving forward, regardless of what happens today.

DAY 75

Memory Verse of the Day

*I have no regrets. I couldn't be more sure
of my ground—the One I've trusted in can
take care of what he's trusted me to do.*

2 TIMOTHY 1:11–12 MSG

LORD, TAKE MY HAND.

God will hold your hand whenever you need Him. He
isn't as impressed with what you do in life as He is
with *how* you tackle each day. He wants you to know
that He's there to take care of you, pick you up when
you fall, and hold you in His loving arms.

*God, teach me Your love. Let me feel
Your embrace. I choose to trust in You.*

DAY 76

Memory Verse of the Day

Create in me a clean heart, O God;
and renew a right spirit within me.

Psalm 51:10 KJV

TIME FOR A MAKEOVER?

Are you feeling sluggish and run-down this morning?
Has your daily routine become a chore? God can fix
that! He has the power to renew your heart and spirit.
All you have to do is ask Him. He'll give you a supreme
spiritual makeover, leaving you feeling refreshed, re-
plenished, and rejuvenated.

Oh God, I need a makeover. Renew my spirit.
Refresh me. Replenish my energy and enthusiasm.

DAY 77

*The LORD my God will help
you do everything needed.*

1 CHRONICLES 28:20 CEV

A LITTLE HELP, PLEASE.

What's on your to-do list today? At times, the list of tasks before you may seem overwhelming. You wonder how you'll ever get them all done. Relax. Take heart. God will give you the strength to do whatever needs to be done today. The rest can wait till tomorrow.

*I put my day in Your hands, Lord.
Guide me in prioritizing my tasks.*

DAY 78

Memory Verse of the Day

*Surely he took up our pain
and bore our suffering.*

ISAIAH 53:4 NIV

HOW CAN I HELP YOU?

Physical pain affects not only the body, but also the spirit. Whether physical pain results from accident, disease, or aging, people sometimes need help keeping their spirits strong. God, of course, is the Great Helper, but you can help too. Look around you today. Is someone hurting? How can you help them?

*Jesus, open my eyes to those who are in physical pain.
Help me to help them put their faith in You.*

DAY 79

*God will generously provide all you need.
Then you will always have everything you
need and plenty left over to share with others.*

2 Corinthians 9:8 nlt

HERE, HAVE SOME OF MINE.

Evaluate your needs against your wants. Can you admit
that because of God's great generosity you have more
than you can use? Share from your abundance today.
Bring joy to someone. You will see more clearly the
folly of seeking security in material possessions, much
of which you don't need anyway.

*Father God, You have blessed me with so
very much! Today I will share it with others.*

DAY 80

Memory Verse of the Day

"I was formed long ages ago, at the very beginning, when the world came to be."

PROVERBS 8:23 NIV

GOD IS ETERNAL.

Men and women come along, filling in a narrow blip of time, and state that all of creation "just simply evolved." Don't let them fool you. God is the Great Creator, He existed before anything else. He designs, plans, and implements all that you see and everything you can't comprehend—both today and forever.

Lord, keep me from taking Your magnificence for granted. Let my heart overflow with gratitude for all You are.

DAY 81

Memory Verse of the Day

For it is God who is at work in you, both to will and to work for His good pleasure.

PHILIPPIANS 2:13 NASB

I CAN BRING GOD PLEASURE.

God finds pleasure working inside of you. Every time you feed the poor, care for the sick, take care of your family, worship at His footstool, spend time with a loved one who's in pain—God is delighted. How wonderful to know that we can bring our Father such pleasure!

Dear heavenly Father, I pray that everything I do today will be pleasing to Your sight.

DAY 82

Memory Verse of the Day

And the LORD shall help them and deliver them;
He shall deliver them from the wicked,
and save them, because they trust in Him.

PSALM 37:40 NKJV

SPECIAL DELIVERY!

The Lord isn't just about delivering you from sin. He also longs to deliver you from selfishness, pain, and many other things that hold you back. He's in the "delivery" business! So what's required from you? Trust. When you place your trust in the Lord, you set yourself up for freedom.

I trust You, Lord. Free me from sin and
everything else that holds me back.

DAY 83

Memory Verse of the Day

I can do all things through
Him who strengthens me.

PHILIPPIANS 4:13 NASB

MISSION POSSIBLE!

It's a brand-new day. Step into it with the attitude that there is nothing—absolutely nothing—you cannot do! There is no "mission impossible" when you are working through Christ. Your potential is limitless, and the possibilities are endless. Christ has already given you the boundless power and strength to succeed.

With You, Lord, I can do anything. Let's go!

DAY 84

Memory Verse of the Day

The LORD himself watches over you! The LORD stands beside you as your protective shade.

PSALM 121:5 NLT

GOD IS MY SPF!

On days when the sun's rays are lethal, you need to be careful not to get burned. Like sunscreen on a hot summer day, God is your SPF (Super Protective Father). Every day He is your ultimate Shelter. With Him always beside you, you'll have it made in the shade. How cool is that?

Thank You for protecting me,
Father, no matter where I am.

DAY 85

Memory Verse of the Day

*You created my inmost being; you knit
me together in my mother's womb.*

PSALM 139:13 NIV

I LOVE WHO I AM.

When you accepted Jesus as your Savior, you became a
whole new person. He is on your side and always will
be. He knows everything there is to know about you,
and He has deemed you worthy of His love. Rejoice in
the truth about who you are in Christ. Embrace the way
God made you.

*Jesus, I love who I am because God
made me and You made me whole.*

DAY 86

Memory Verse of the Day

They sow the wind and they reap the whirlwind.

HOSEA 8:7 NASB

LIFT UP MY FAITH, LORD.

Wind can be gale-force strong or as soft as a puff of air; devastating or beneficial. Whether a gentle breeze or a whirlwind, it is under God's authority. Today's verse illustrates the destruction that comes from disobedience. Be careful not to put your faith in worldly things. Remember who controls the wind.

Lift my faith, Lord, lift it as if on eagle's wings, soaring high above worldly things.

DAY 87

Memory Verse of the Day

*Whatsoever ye do, do it heartily,
as to the Lord and not unto men.*

COLOSSIANS 3:23 KJV

GOD IS THE BOSS OF ME!

It's easy to forget who your real boss is, especially in a demanding environment. No matter where you work, God wants you to do your work wholeheartedly, even when no one is looking. By pleasing God in all you say and do, others will see Him through your work ethic.

*God, keep reminding me that You are
my boss. My goal at work is to please You.*

DAY 88

Memory Verse of the Day

*And even though you do not see [Jesus] now,
you believe in him and are filled with
an inexpressible and glorious joy.*

1 PETER 1:8 NIV 1984

THERE IS JOY IN SALVATION.

Joy comes as a result of whom you trust, not in what you have. Joy is Jesus. When you find Jesus, "all things become new" as the Bible promises, and once again you view the world through a child's eyes. Excitedly, you experience the "inexpressible and glorious joy" that salvation brings.

*Father, thank You for sending Jesus to save me.
Thank You for the joy that comes with salvation.*

DAY 89

I call on you, O God, for you will answer me;
give ear to me and hear my prayer.

PSALM 17:6 NIV 1984

GOD IS ALWAYS AVAILABLE.

God can be reached at any hour of the day or night and every day of the year—including weekends and holidays! When you pray, you don't have to worry about disconnections, hang-ups, or poor reception. You will never be put on hold, nor will your prayers be diverted to another department. God is always available.

How wonderful it is, Lord, to know that You
are always accessible to me, for whatever
I need, twenty-four hours a day.

DAY 90

Memory Verse of the Day

"But he who enters by the door is a shepherd of the sheep. To him the doorkeeper opens, and the sheep hear his voice, and he calls his own sheep by name and leads them out."

JOHN 10:2–3 NASB

HE KNOWS MY NAME.

God knows your name. He knows and calls you by name, just as a shepherd knows and calls each of his sheep. God's relationship with you is unique as He leads you through life. Someday, when the Good Shepherd calls you home to heaven, you'll hear Him speak your name. Won't that be wonderful?

Good Shepherd, among all the people in the world, You know me by name. Our relationship is loving and unique. How amazing!

DAY 91

Memory Verse of the Day

Since we live by the Spirit,
let us keep in step with the Spirit.

GALATIANS 5:25 NIV

HELP! I'M STUCK!

Picture yourself stuck in quicksand, unable to move forward or backward. Not a very pleasant feeling, is it? There's good news today! God's Word promises that you have the capability of reaching forward to what lies ahead. Focus on the Spirit, and allow Him to pull you out of the sand!

Father, I feel stuck! Please help me to get
out of this place and start moving forward.

DAY 92

Memory Verse of the Day

He put a new song in my mouth, a song of
praise to our God. Many people will see this
and worship him. Then they will trust the LORD.

PSALM 40:3 NCV

I WILL PRAISE HIM WITH SINGING.

Do you love to sing? God promises to put a song in your
mouth, and not just any song—He wants this joyous
chorus to bubble up inside of you so that many will
hear it and trust God, just like you do. Start warming
up that voice right now!

Lord, I will praise You with singing.

DAY 93

Memory Verse of the Day

*"People look at the outward appearance,
but the Lord looks at the heart."*

1 Samuel 16:7 niv

GOD THINKS THE WORLD OF ME!

Do you struggle with issues such as insecurity, body image, a desire for love, and other worldly things? The standard for measure is usually the world's standards. Think about it: How can you be concerned about what the world thinks when the Creator of the universe thinks the world of you?

Heavenly Father, that You think the world of me is all that matters. Thank You! I love You.

DAY 94

Memory Verse of the Day

The tongue has the power of life and death.

PROVERBS 18:21 NIV

SAY WHAT?

Today, think about your words. Words can bring you down to the depths of despair. Despite what you know about God's grace, you can destroy your confidence and joy by participating in negative talk. It grieves the heart of God to hear His children slip under the weight of harmful words.

Dear Lord, remind me to be mindful of my words today. Let my speech be pleasing to You.

DAY 95

Memory Verse of the Day

*"Arise! For this matter is your responsibility,
but we will be with you; be courageous and act."*

EZRA 10:4 NASB

RAH! RAH! RAH!

Facing unexpected responsibility might fray your nerves. Fortunately, you can find the courage to act when others cheer you on and promise you support. Remember this: God is the leader of your cheering section. Seek friends and family to cheer you on. Be brave. Do what needs to be done!

Lord, I will rise and act in Your strength!

DAY 96

Memory Verse of the Day

*May [God] give you the power to accomplish
all the good things your faith prompts you to do.*

2 Thessalonians 1:11 nlt

POWER UP!

It's time to power up for the day. God has already
equipped you with the power to accomplish whatever
your faith is calling you to do. What an awesome boost
to your self-assurance! Start the day with this verse,
and you will have confidence in everything. Walk
tall, walk strong!

*Lord, I walk confident that Your
power is surging through me.*

DAY 97

Memory Verse of the Day

When you become successful, don't say, "I'm rich, and I've earned it all myself." Instead, remember that the LORD your God gives you the strength to make a living.

DEUTERONOMY 8:17–18 CEV

I'M RICH! NOW WHAT?

Riches don't impress God. He created everything we have, and it all belongs to Him. He can give a vast fortune and snatch it away just as easily. Instead of reveling in financial success, we should remember what an honor it is to serve as ambassadors for God's kingdom.

Father, never allow me to become self-satisfied from success. I know that all I have comes from You.

DAY 98

Memory Verse of the Day

Since we have so great a cloud of witnesses surrounding us, let us also lay aside every encumbrance and the sin which so easily entangles us.

Hebrews 12:1 nasb

FIND WHAT'S HIDDEN.

It's easy to recognize your obvious sins and undesirable thoughts. But what about the less obvious, sometimes even cherished, thoughts and habits that you hang on to? The Bible instructs you to discard anything that hinders your faith. Your heavenly Father supplies the courage and strength you need to do just that.

Lord, open my eyes today to anything hidden that gets in the way of my faith.

DAY 99

*And my God shall supply all your need
according to His riches in glory by Christ Jesus.*

PHILIPPIANS 4:19 NKJV

GOD'S GOT IT COVERED.

God promises to meet your needs. That means you don't have to fret over where the next meal or set of clothing you need is coming from. He's got it covered—in His time and His own unique way. So, no worries. God, who owns the cattle on a thousand hills, can certainly meet your needs.

*Father God, thank You for supplying all
of my needs, each and every day.*

DAY 100

Memory Verse of the Day

Even though I walk through the darkest valley,
I will fear no evil, for you are with me; your
rod and your staff, they comfort me.

PSALM 23:4 NIV

GOD IS HERE!

When God shows up in a situation, fear disappears in an instant. Does that mean that the "situation" instantly disappears? No, it doesn't. But knowing that the Lord is there with His arms around you will help so much. The journey through life's valleys is bearable when you're not alone.

Put Your arms around me, Lord. Hold me up.
Let's walk through this valley together.

DAY 101

Memory Verse of the Day

*"For the mountains may depart and the
hills be removed, but my steadfast love
shall not depart from you, and my covenant
of peace shall not be removed," says the LORD,
who has compassion on you.*

ISAIAH 54:10 ESV

GOD'S LOVE IS STEADFAST.

Mountains are steadfast and immovable. Even small
parts are not easily budged. Nature's forces take cen-
turies or tremendous energy to move. God says that His
love is even more immovable. Mountains will move before His love will leave you. Hills will depart more easily
than God would remove His covenant of peace from you.

*Father, thank You for Your immovable love,
for the permanence of Your covenant of peace.*

DAY 102

Memory Verse of the Day

*Don't be concerned about the outward beauty
of fancy hairstyles, expensive jewelry, or beautiful
clothes. You should clothe yourselves instead with the
beauty that comes from within, the unfading beauty of
a gentle and quiet spirit, which is so precious to God.*

1 Peter 3:3–4 nlt

WHAT SHALL I WEAR?

While fashion trends are fun, you shouldn't forget
where true beauty comes from. It was Jesus who taught
us not to place our treasure in physical things like
our bodies, nor worry about where we get our clothes.
Jesus will transform your spirit from rags to riches
because He loves you.

Dear Jesus, I feel beautiful because You love me!

DAY 103

Memory Verse of the Day

If anyone is in Christ, he is a new creation;
old things have passed away; behold,
all things have become new.

2 Corinthians 5:17 nkjv

HE MAKES ALL THINGS NEW.

To "become" new implies an ongoing action. We are new in Jesus every day of our lives. The old, unproductive things drop away, leaving us with our regenerating life with Christ. When we grab hold of this truth, our eyes are opened to see what new things He has for us each day.

Open my eyes, Jesus! What do You
have for me on this brand-new day?

DAY 104

Memory Verse of the Day

"In this world you will have trouble.
But take heart! I have overcome the world."

John 16:33 niv

HE MAKES ALL THINGS NEW.

Troubling events in the world might rob you of your sense of security and well-being. The rapid decline of morality, integrity, and godliness might make you question God and wonder why He doesn't fix everything. You need to remember that God is your Fortress—and He has already won the battle.

Thank You, Lord, for reminding me that You have a battle plan, and that You will win the war.

DAY 105

Memory Verse of the Day

"Well done, good and faithful servant! You have been faithful with a few things; I will put you in charge of many things. Come and share your master's happiness!"

MATTHEW 25:21 NIV

IT'S A WIN-WIN SITUATION.

Make a list of things you do well, and ask God which ones He wants you to use in service to Him. When you use your talents, God rewards you for your efforts, invites you to share in His joy, and gives you a promotion to boot! It's a win-win situation.

I am Your servant, Lord.
Show me what You want me to do.

DAY 106

Memory Verse of the Day

I praise the LORD because he advises me.
Even at night, I feel his leading.

PSALM 16:7 NCV

TODAY WILL BE AWESOME!

Get ready for an awesome day! You know it will be great because God is your Adviser. Throughout the day, if only you will listen to His whisperings, He will impart wisdom and lead you forward in great and amazing ways. Now, get out there and have a God-filled, awesome day!

Lord, I praise You! Thank You for
leading me with Your wisdom.

DAY 107

Memory Verse of the Day

[Jesus said,] "I came so they can have real and eternal life, more and better life than they ever dreamed of."

JOHN 10:10 MSG

SMILE!

You have been blessed with an abundant life. That should put a smile on your face. So, show the world! Make it a point today to smile at everyone you meet. Say a friendly, "Hello." Allow God's light to radiate through you. You'll be surprised by those who smile back.

My Savior Jesus, You have given me the ultimate reason to smile. Help me to share that joy with others.

DAY 108

Memory Verse of the Day

*"Come to me, all you who are weary
and burdened, and I will give you rest."*

MATTHEW 11:28 NIV

I NEED A BREAK!

Are you overdue for a break? If so, ask the Lord to show you how you can take Him up on this promise: That you can come to Him (weary and heavy-laden) and experience true rest and refreshment. He will do it! You simply have to take the time to meet Him there. Ah, rest!

*Dear Father God, I'm worn out. I need a break.
Here I am, Lord. Grant me Your rest.*

Memory Verse of the Day

But as many as received Him, to them He gave the right to become children of God, to those who believe in His name.

JOHN 1:12 NKJV

BUT I'M A GROWN-UP!

You might be a grown-up, but to God, you are one of His kids. Imagine how He must feel when He gazes into your face. What joy it must bring your heavenly Father to dote on you, to care for your every need, and to provide you with infinite blessings.

I sometimes forget, God, that You see me as a child still in need of Your guidance. Thank You for being my loving Father.

DAY 110

Memory Verse of the Day

And these things happened as examples for us, to stop us from wanting evil things as those people did.

1 Corinthians 10:6 ncv

I CAN LEARN FROM GOD'S PEOPLE.

By reading the Bible, you will learn from God's dealings with people throughout history not to fall into the same traps. Twenty-three thousand died in one day because they worshipped pagan gods, refusing to obey the one true God. As you read about people and their struggles in God's Word, learn from them.

I am discovering, God, that the Bible is full of examples that apply to my own life. Thank You for them.

DAY 111

Memory Verse of the Day

There is no distinction between Greek and Jew,
circumcised and uncircumcised, barbarian, Scythian,
slave and freeman, but Christ is all, and in all.

COLOSSIANS 3:11 NASB

LET'S ALL GET ALONG.

Is there prejudice in your heart? To say you love Jesus
and yet maintain deeply rooted prejudices against
others is inconsistent with everything He taught. Jesus
came to reconcile all people to Himself, not separate
them into factions. We all belong to God. Remember
that today. Open your heart to others.

Dear Lord, if there is any prejudice in my heart,
make me aware, and wash it away.

DAY 112

Memory Verse of the Day

*"This is its meaning: The seed
is God's message to men."*

LUKE 8:11 TLB

GOD'S WORD IS IN MY HEART.

Each scripture verse you memorize is like a seed God plants in your heart. Whether or not it grows depends on you. Are you thinking about the verses as you memorize them? Are you applying them to your life? If so, then the seed God planted is growing—and so is your faith!

Father, I will learn and meditate on the scriptures You give me. I will apply them to my life.

DAY 113

Memory Verse of the Day

You are complete in Him, who is the
head of all principality and power.

COLOSSIANS 2:10 NKJV

JESUS COMPLETES ME.

Imagine what life would be like if you had no awareness of Jesus' power and desire to provide everything that you need to reflect His glory. His offer of the opportunity to be complete in Him is a genuine demonstration of what He is prepared to share with you—which is everything!

Jesus, like that movie cliché goes: "You complete me!"
Thank You for being my everything.

DAY 114

Memory Verse of the Day

*But Jesus often withdrew to
lonely places and prayed.*

LUKE 5:16 NIV

SOLITUDE IS GOOD.

You are God's hands and feet in this world, and He can use you in mighty ways. But He also calls you to rest and pray. Jesus put a priority on this, frequently leaving the crowd to seek solitude. He encourages you to do the same. Make quiet prayer your priority today.

*Father, allow me to say no to something today
so that I might say yes to quiet time with You.*

DAY 115

Memory Verse of the Day

For I, the LORD your God, hold your
right hand; it is I who say to you,
"Fear not, I am the one who helps you."

ISAIAH 41:13 ESV

MY HAND IN GOD'S.

God holds your hand. He protects you and comforts you.
He is with you in your most anxious moments and in
your darkest hours. With the clasp of His hand comes
courage for any situation. He tells you not to be afraid.
Why? Because He has a hold on you.

Almighty God, I am grateful that You hold my hand.
Forgive me for the times when I have forgotten
this and allowed fear to reign in my life.

DAY 116

Memory Verse of the Day

"I am the Lord, and I do not change."

Malachi 3:6 nlt

GOD DOES NOT CHANGE.

In this world, change is the one thing you can count on. But God is not of this world. He is supernatural, other-worldly. And He does not change. His strength, saving grace, and power are a sure thing no matter where, no matter when. Count on it! Count on Him today.

What a relief, God,
that I can always depend on You.

DAY 117

"You keep him in perfect peace whose mind is stayed on you, because he trusts in you."

ISAIAH 26:3 ESV

HIS PEACE IS PERFECT.

When your eyes are on God, everything else fades to gray—problems seem smaller, enemies weaker, and sorrows dimmer. If your eyes are fixed only on Him, you will experience a peace beyond all understanding. Focus on God today. And if you find yourself slipping out of focus, ask Him to reset your sight.

All-powerful God, help me to see clearly today by focusing my thoughts on You.

DAY 118

Memory Verse of the Day

Put on the full armor of God, so that. . .you may be able to stand your ground, and after you have done everything, to stand.

EPHESIANS 6:13 NIV

GOD'S ARMOR PROTECTS ME.

The Bible says that God's armor is the belt of truth, the breastplate of righteousness, a fitting for your feet of readiness that comes from the Gospel of peace, the shield of faith, and the helmet of salvation. Put on His armor before you leave the house today, and nothing—nothing!—can harm you.

With all Your armor covering me, God, I am ready for anything. Thank You!

DAY 119

Memory Verse of the Day

The righteous lead blameless lives;
blessed are their children after them.

<small>PROVERBS 20:7 NIV</small>

HOW CAN I BLESS MY CHILDREN?

Want to know the best possible way to bless your children? Live a righteous life. When you live a life pleasing to God, He is watching—and blessing. You are leaving a very special legacy for your children, and this makes Him happy. He, in turn, bestows blessing upon blessing.

God, help me to set the best example for my
children by living in a way that is pleasing to You.

DAY 120

Memory Verse of the Day

*"For I will forgive their wickedness and
will remember their sins no more."*
HEBREWS 8:12 NIV

FORGIVE AND FORGET.

How can God—the All-Knowing—not only forgive, but possibly forget our sins? He promises to do so. If only we could forget when we forgive others for the things they've done to wound us. What a blissful situation, to have no recollection of the past wrongs done to us.

*God, help me not only to forgive those who have
harmed me, but also to put it out of my mind.*

DAY 121

Memory Verse of the Day

*"Until now you have not asked for anything
in my name. Ask and you will receive,
and your joy will be complete."*

JOHN 16:24 NIV

I ASK IN JESUS' NAME.

Asking in Jesus' name puts you in line with His will,
what your wants should be, and what your needs
really are. With a Christlike mind, you are more likely
to want the best things, the right things. This is what
brings the joy—knowing you are one with Christ in
your desires.

*God, for what I have asked of You,
in Jesus' name I pray. Amen.*

DAY 122

Memory Verse of the Day

My eyes are always on the LORD, for he rescues me from the traps of my enemies.

PSALM 25:15 NLT

I WILL FOLLOW JESUS.

When your concentration strays from Jesus, you risk going your own way and falling into the enemy's traps. Jesus wants to show you the safe path, the one that goes around the enemy of your soul. He walks ahead of you, looking back to see if you are following Him— so follow Him today!

Jesus, I pray that when You look behind You today, You will see me following You.

DAY 123

*See then that ye walk circumspectly,
not as fools, but as wise, redeeming
the time, because the days are evil.*

EPHESIANS 5:15–16 KJV

I WILL TELL OTHERS ABOUT JESUS.

Tell someone about Jesus today. Your primary desire should be to help people know Him. This doesn't mean that all you ever do is talk about God, but when He gives you opportunities, you should take them. No matter what you do or say, your actions should always set a Christlike example.

*Dear God, open up opportunities today for me
to share Jesus with my coworkers and friends.*

DAY 124

*"Hold tight to God, your God,
just as you've done up to now."*

Joshua 23:8 msg

DON'T LET GO!

Sometimes life might come at you so fast that you just want to give up. Hang on with faith. Don't let go! The enemy of your soul wants you to quit. You've gotten this far in your faith believing that God will keep His promises and help you reach your destiny. Don't stop now.

*Father God, when I feel like quitting,
take my hand and lead me.*

DAY 125

Memory Verse of the Day

"If you forgive others for their transgressions, your heavenly Father will also forgive you."

MATTHEW 6:14 NASB

HURT HAPPENS.

People may hurt you without meaning to. Often, their offense is hurtful to them too. God wants you to show mercy to the person who caused the pain. A gentle response is a reflection of God's character. He provided you with the ability to forgive because He forgave *you*. Whom do you need to forgive today?

Lord God, help me to forgive _____ today.
And thank You for forgiving me!

DAY 126

Memory Verse of the Day

You are of God. . . . He who is in you is greater than he who is in the world.

1 John 4:4 nkjv

CELEBRATE!

You have something to celebrate today—and every day: The Spirit of God lives within you, right now and always! Nothing in this world—people, problems, evils, losses, greed, grief, terror—is mightier than Him! Plant that thought deep in your mind this morning, and your confidence, your spirit, will thrive!

Heavenly Father, today I will celebrate Your greatness. Thank You for making Your home in my heart.

DAY 127

Memory Verse of the Day

"When you pass through the waters, I will be with you; and through the rivers, they shall not overflow you. When you walk through the fire, you shall not be burned, nor shall the flame scorch you."

ISAIAH 43:2 NKJV

THROUGH IT ALL. . .

God doesn't promise that you won't have problems. But He does promise to be with you when you do. He is by your side, keeping you afloat in the "flood." He'll keep you from getting burned in the "fire." He is the One who will never, ever leave you. That's true love!

Thank You, God, for always being by my side. I know I can count on You!

DAY 128

Freely (without pay) you have received,
freely (without charge) give.
MATTHEW 10:8 AMPC

FREELY I HAVE RECEIVED.

God has given you so many gifts. He gives you love and affection to keep you moving in a righteous direction. Everything you are, everything you have, has been given to you by God, overflowing and free. Share His gifts with others today, and trust that God will continue to provide.

Thank You, God, for Your precious gifts.
Be with me, now, as I give to others.

DAY 129

*Yet he did not waver through unbelief
regarding the promise of God, but was
strengthened in his faith and gave glory
to God, being fully persuaded that God
had power to do what he had promised.*

ROMANS 4:20–21 NIV

I'M GROWING!

Just like children grow and change, Christians also grow
as believers. Your spiritual growth depends on spending
time in God's Word and praying. How fun, to think that
you're growing in your faith! How pleased God must be
when He looks at the changes going on in your heart
and life.

*Heavenly Father, every day I feel our
relationship becoming stronger. I love
this growing, changing process!*

DAY 130

Memory Verse of the Day

"Those who hate you will be clothed with shame, and the dwelling place of the wicked will come to nothing."

JOB 8:22 NKJV

SHAME, SHAME, SHAME!

Those who love the Lord are "dressed" in His finest (joy, peace, strength, and so on). Today's verse says that those who oppose God's ways will be clothed in shame. They will wear shame like a cloak. So, if someone does you wrong, don't worry. God will put them to shame!

God, I give to You all the insults and wrongdoings done to me by others. Shame them, if You please.

DAY 131

Memory Verse of the Day

"It is the Lord who goes before you."

DEUTERONOMY 31:8 ESV

THE LORD GOES BEFORE ME.

When you are heading into unknown territory, it's a relief to know that someone has gone ahead of you to secure your destination. A guide is of great value to someone unsure of what might lie ahead. The Lord is your Guide. Ask Him to go before you today.

Lord, I don't know what lies ahead,
but You do. Guide me to it and through it.

DAY 132

Because of his glory and excellence, he has
given us great and precious promises.

2 Peter 1:4 nlt

GOD KEEPS HIS WORD.

People may let you down, but God never will. His Word
offers hundreds of promises, and He is more than able
to deliver them. God's motivation is love, which is the
very definition of who He is. God cannot fail, He will
not disappoint, and He does what He says He will do.

Dear Father, I praise You because You
never disappoint. You never let me down.

DAY 133

Memory Verse of the Day

Jesus replied: " 'Love the Lord your God with all your heart and with all your soul and with all your mind.' This is the first and greatest commandment. And the second is like it: 'Love your neighbor as yourself.' "

MATTHEW 22:37–39 NIV

I WALK THE "LOVE TALK."

When you say, "I love you," do you mean it? Telling someone you love them and showing love are two very different things. Let's face it—some people are harder to love than others. But God wants us to walk the "love talk" always, not just when we want to or when it's convenient.

Lord, I promise to love You and my neighbor with my whole heart.

DAY 134

Memory Verse of the Day

The Lord bless thee, and keep thee;
the Lord make his face shine upon thee,
and be gracious unto thee.

Numbers 6:24–25 kjv

BLESS HIS HOLY NAME.

Once you have a relationship with God the Father through Jesus Christ, you are in line for a multitude of blessings. God's love for you is eternal, as are His gifts. So open your arms and become a thankful recipient for all He's given. Praise Him and bless His holy name.

Lord, You have given me so much, and I am
thankful. Let me give thanks for Your gifts.

DAY 135

Memory Verse of the Day

The LORD their God will save his people on that day as a shepherd saves his flock. They will sparkle in his land like jewels in a crown.

ZECHARIAH 9:16 NIV

I AM A JEWEL. . .

When you accepted Christ, you became a crown jewel! With divine precision, He painstakingly chiseled away the ugly rough spots. He applied heat and pressure for your clarity, and then polished you until you glistened. Jesus created you as a gemstone from crude rock, forming a jewel worthy of a setting in His crown.

Jesus, thank You for saving me. You accepted me just as I was and made me into a crown jewel!

DAY 136

Memory Verse of the Day

*If we walk in the Light as He Himself is in the Light,
we have fellowship with one another, and the
blood of Jesus His Son cleanses us from all sin.*

1 John 1:7 nasb

WHAT IF THE LIGHTS GO OUT?

Losing faith in God is like a power outage—nothing
works and it's hard to see. But when you live in submission to His authority, He will light your way. With the
Lord at your side, you have no reason to fear a power
outage. . .today, and every day, God is your Light.

*Almighty God, my day is in Your hands.
I trust You to be my Light and to guide me.*

DAY 137

Memory Verse of the Day

David was greatly distressed because
the men were talking of stoning him. . . .
But David found strength in the LORD his God.

1 SAMUEL 30:6 NIV

I WILL TRUST IN GOD.

Are you upset about what someone said? When hurtful, worrisome words echo in your ears, drown them out with a prayer to God Almighty. He will give you strength and shield you from the slings and arrows of others. Like David in today's memory verse, put your trust in Him.

Lord, fill my mind with Your good words
and my heart with Your awesome strength.

DAY 138

Memory Verse of the Day

Wait for the LORD; be strong and let your heart take courage; yes, wait for the LORD.

PSALM 27:14 NASB

I WILL WAIT FOR HIM.

Courage is framed by patience in the Lord and trust that He will bring about what He has promised in your life. If you feel like running on ahead of Him, wait—and wait some more. If you dig into your ensured expectation that His promises will be realized, then your courage will grow.

As I walk by faith, Lord, I become stronger every day.

DAY 139

Memory Verse of the Day

Anxiety weighs down the heart,
but a kind word cheers it up.

PROVERBS 12:25 NIV

WORDS. . .WORDS. . .WORDS!

What kind of words are you speaking to yourself and others? Words of kindness, or sharp, critical ones? Words can build up or tear down. God didn't put humans on earth to cut others down or to offer critique. His Holy Spirit does a far better job correcting people. Speak only kind words today!

Dear God, today I will watch my words
and use them to build others up.

DAY 140

"The eternal God is your refuge, and underneath are the everlasting arms; He will thrust out the enemy from before you, and will say, 'Destroy!' "

DEUTERONOMY 33:27 NKJV

GOD IS MY SAFE PLACE.

Imagine your ultimate dream home—your "safe" place to dwell. Then remember this: The very safest—and most luxurious—place to live is in God's presence. How do you get there? By spending time with Him. In that place, He provides comfort, security, joy, peace, and all of the other things you need.

Father God, You are my safe place. I know that in Your presence, I have all that I need.

DAY 141

Memory Verse of the Day

*Having predestined us to adoption
as sons by Jesus Christ to Himself,
according to the good pleasure of His will.*

EPHESIANS 1:5 NKJV

WHO AM I, REALLY?

Have you ever wondered, *Who am I, really?* Like an adopted child, you are chosen. Even before the foundation of the world was set in place, God chose *you* to be His child. He created you for His pleasure and brought you into His family for your blessing. That's who you are—really!

*God, when I question my identity,
remind me of what really matters—I am Yours!*

DAY 142

Memory Verse of the Day

*He who is joined to the Lord
is one spirit with Him.*

1 Corinthians 6:17 nkjv

OUR RELATIONSHIP IS ETERNAL.

Human relationships are fragile and too often broken by circumstances. Even the best earthly union is only valid until death. But our union with Christ is, in the deepest sense, an unbreakable, lasting covenant. The joy and strength you receive from joining your spirit with the living God lasts through eternity.

*Almighty God, how wonderful it is
to know that You and I are forever!*

DAY 143

Memory Verse of the Day

Why are you downcast, O my soul? Why so
disturbed within me? Put your hope in God,
for I will yet praise him, my Savior and my God.

<small>PSALM 42:5–6 NIV1984</small>

I HOPE. . .

When circumstances make you feel depressed, remember that you have hope. Hope that your circumstances will not always be the way they are right now. Hope that no matter how dismal your situation seems, God is in control, and He will win this battle for you. Allow yourself to hope today!

Father, when I am discouraged, I will remember that
You are in control of the situation—You are still God!

DAY 144

Memory Verse of the Day

*Because of the LORD's great love we
are not consumed, for his compassions
never fail. They are new every morning;
great is your faithfulness.*

LAMENTATIONS 3:22–23 NIV

TODAY IS A NEW BEGINNING.

God starts out His day offering renewed compassion
to His children. No matter what trials, difficulties, and
sins yesterday brought, the morning ushers in a fresh
experience, a brand-new beginning for believers who
seek His forgiveness. All you have to do is accept His
gift. Today is a brand-new day!

*God, Your promise of never-ending compassion
for me is amazing! I never want to take for
granted the grace You offer every day.*

DAY 145

*"Yet even now," declares the L*ORD*, "return to Me with all your heart, and with fasting, weeping and mourning; and rend your heart and not your garments."*

JOEL 2:12–13 NASB

HE RESTORES MY RIGHTEOUSNESS.

When you stray from God's path of righteousness, He asks that you return to Him with a contrite heart, mind, and soul. His abundant love does more than patch a heart ripped open by regret. His mercy restores it. You are His, patched and mended, because of His great love for you.

Father God, I've made a mess of things. Please forgive me, and help me not to do it again!

DAY 146

Memory Verse of the Day

Do not let this one fact escape your notice, beloved,
that with the Lord one day is like a thousand years,
and a thousand years like one day.

2 Peter 3:8 nasb

GOD CREATED TIME.

Two thousand years have passed since Peter wrote about Christ's anticipated return. But it's only been a day in heaven, maybe two. We can't comprehend God's calendar. Infinity is a mystery. Although God dwells in eternity, He created time for us here on earth. So make the most of your time today.

Lord, time is Your precious gift.
Remind me to make the most of it today.

DAY 147

Memory Verse of the Day

*"Whoever believes in me, as Scripture has said,
rivers of living water will flow from within them."*

JOHN 7:38 NIV

LIVING WATER.

Moving water has the power to shape rocks, mountains, and valleys. Today's memory verse says that Christ within you is a continual, unstoppable force of living water, molding you, feeding you, directing you, and putting a spring of joy in your step! Walk joyfully today with God at your side.

*Today, Jesus, I will remember that You
dwell within me. Guide me. Teach me.*

DAY 148

Memory Verse of the Day

"Do to others as you would like them to do to you."
LUKE 6:31 NLT

I WILL DO UNTO OTHERS.

Today's scripture verse is also known as the Golden Rule. What a wonderful world this would be if everyone treated others like they'd want to be treated. Such a movement can become a reality, and it can begin with you. Follow this Golden Rule today, and see how it makes you feel.

Help me to follow Your Golden Rule, Lord!

DAY 149

Memory Verse of the Day

*"For those who exalt themselves will be humbled,
and those who humble themselves will be exalted."*

<small>MATTHEW 23:12 NIV</small>

AWAY WITH YOU, PRIDE!

We talk about humility, but do we live it? No one sets out to be prideful, but it's difficult not to put personal needs and desires first. Still, when we humble ourselves and focus on others, God lifts us up. He does a far better job of exalting than we could ever do!

*God, forgive me for those times when I
have been prideful. I come to You
now with a humble heart.*

DAY 150

Memory Verse of the Day

Do not let sin have power over you.
Let good have power over sin!
ROMANS 12:21 NLV

GOOD WINS OVER EVIL.

As a believer, you might argue that you are rarely "overcome" by sin and evil. However, there are days when your temper gets the best of you or you get overwhelmed. That's how the enemy catches you off guard and pulls you off course. Today, be aware of his tactics. Be prepared.

Open my eyes, Lord, to sin,
and help me to fight it at every turn.

DAY 151

Memory Verse of the Day

Commit to the LORD whatever you do,
and he will establish your plans.

PROVERBS 16:3 NIV

GOD IS MY ARCHITECT.

God is the great Architect of your life, and He has a cus-tom life-plan just for you. Allowing Him to plan your life is never a risk, because He already knows exactly what you need. That was established even before you were born. God's plan is perfect for you.

Lord, help me not to get in the way of Your work.
I'm eager to see what You have planned for me.

DAY 152

Memory Verse of the Day

It is good for me that I have been afflicted,
that I may learn Your statutes.

PSALM 119:71 NKJV

SHOULD I PLAY IT SAFE?

Everything has gone according to your plans. You face no resistance to what you want for your life because you've played it safe and taken no risks, eliminating any possibility of discomfort. But—think about it—we grow when we take risks and experience roadblocks. God uses them to deepen our faith.

Father God, it's easy to be comfortable where
I'm at, but where do You want me to go?

DAY 153

Memory Verse of the Day

Love from the center of who you are;
don't fake it. Run for dear life from evil;
hold on for dear life to good. Be good friends
who love deeply; practice playing second fiddle.

ROMANS 12:9–10 MSG

LOVE WITH A GENUINE HEART.

The Message uses the metaphor, "practice playing second fiddle," to help us understand how we should honor one another. We should take the second part, putting others before ourselves, encouraging them with love and devotion. If you love without hypocrisy and honor others above yourself, you will help make the world a better place.

Dear Lord, please help me to love with a genuine heart and to take second place to those around me.

DAY 154

Memory Verse of the Day

"This vision is for a future time. It describes the end, and it will be fulfilled. If it seems slow in coming, wait patiently, for it will surely take place. It will not be delayed."

HABAKKUK 2:3 NLT

GOD, I'M WAITING.

What are you waiting for today? Sometimes the things you're waiting for might come slowly. Similarly, God's plans might come slowly, but they come steadily, surely. God is going to do what He says He'll do. You won't know when, exactly, but God wants you to be faithful while you wait.

Lord, I'm used to things moving really fast. Help me to wait patiently and faithfully.

DAY 155

Memory Verse of the Day

*"Call to me and I will answer you. I'll tell
you marvelous and wondrous things that
you could never figure out on your own."*

Jeremiah 33:3 MSG

GOD HAS ALL THE ANSWERS.

Where can you go to find answers to your deepest questions? When you need discernment, wisdom, or insight into a situation, God is never further than a prayer away. He, the Source of all knowledge, will give you the inside scoop. He'll tell you things you never imagined. That's divine inspiration!

*I come to You in prayer, Lord,
seeking Your knowledge. Fill me up!*

DAY 156

Memory Verse of the Day

*"You will. . .clear out the old
[to make room] for the new."*
LEVITICUS 26:10 AMP

IS IT TIME TO MOVE ON?

There are times when something you once loved doing
seems more like a burden than a blessing. It may be time
to relinquish the old and begin a new endeavor. But, as
in all things, before making that decision, ask the Lord
for guidance. He'll steer you in the right direction.

*Father, I've become weary of _____. Guide me.
Shall I stick with it, or start something new?*

DAY 157

Memory Verse of the Day

"For God did not send his Son into the world to condemn the world, but in order that the world might be saved through him."

JOHN 3:17 ESV

NO COMMENT.

You will make mistakes (we all do), but God doesn't stand over you, clucking His tongue and saying, "Can't you get anything right?" When you come to Him, accepting His gift of salvation, all of the icky stuff (worthy of critique) is washed away. There's nothing left to comment on!

Oh Father God, thank You for forgiving me and washing away my sins.

DAY 158

Be happy in the Lord. And He will give you the desires of your heart.

Psalm 37:4 nlv

GOD CARES ABOUT WHAT I WANT.

God cares very much about the desires of your heart. He longs to see you giddy with delight over the blessings He can bestow. So if you really want to benefit from all that the Lord has in store, make up your mind to be happy/content, no matter what.

Almighty Father, as I go about my work today, fill my heart with happiness.

DAY 159

Memory Verse of the Day

*Since God chose you to be the holy people
he loves, you must clothe yourselves with
tenderhearted mercy, kindness, humility,
gentleness, and patience.*

Colossians 3:12 nlt

PUT ON YOUR GODLY CLOTHES!

Think about the attributes of God outlined in today's
verse. It's your responsibility to put on this "godly attire"
every morning. As you get dressed, you can intention-
ally decide to wear His attributes so others can see
those qualities that characterize God's holiness—and, by
extension, the qualities He graces you with as well.

*Lord, I will dress myself this morning in tenderhearted
mercy, kindness, humility, gentleness, and patience.*

DAY 160

Don't worry about anything; instead, pray about everything. Tell God what you need, and thank him for all he has done.

Philippians 4:6 NLT

DON'T WORRY ABOUT IT.

"Don't worry about it." How many times have you heard that? Don't worry. It's easier said than done. But that is exactly what God wants you to do. When you put aside your worries, believing that He has everything under control, you show your faith in Him, and He will reward you.

God, I know that You have my problems under control, so please help me not to worry.

DAY 161

Memory Verse of the Day

"Catch for us the foxes, the little foxes that ruin the vineyards."

SONG OF SOLOMON 2:15 NIV

AWAY WITH YOU, LITTLE FOXES!

The Bible teaches that the "little foxes" in life "spoil the vine." Little foxes are the trivial, petty annoyances you encounter daily. One or two consecutive foxes can hurl you into an all-out tailspin, ruining an otherwise perfect day. So watch out for those little foxes today, and shoo them away.

Dear God, please give comfort to my disquieted soul and drive away the little foxes of aggravation.

DAY 162

Memory Verse of the Day

*Our bodies. . .were made for the Lord,
and the Lord cares about our bodies.*

1 CORINTHIANS 6:13 NLT

GOD CARES ABOUT MY HEALTH.

Your body is a temple of the Most High God! He cares about how you take care of—or neglect—yourself. Today, be mindful of how you rest, work, eat, move, and play. Begin to sense what things are beneficial to your overall health and to the maintenance of your body—God's temple.

Lord, make me aware today of how I care for my body. Help me to remember that it is Your temple.

DAY 163

Memory Verse of the Day

Now may the Lord of peace Himself continually grant you peace in every circumstance. The Lord be with you all!

2 Thessalonians 3:16 nasb

GOD'S GIFT OF PEACE.

One of God's greatest gifts to humankind is peace, and it is yours for the asking. In every trial and amid all of life's traumas, peace will reign in your mind, body, and soul if you are abiding in Jesus. Remain in Him and all will be well. Think about that today.

Dear God, fill me with Your abundant, life-giving peace.

DAY 164

Memory Verse of the Day

*So roll up your sleeves, get your head in the game,
be totally ready to receive the gift that's
coming when Jesus arrives.*

1 Peter 1:13 msg

GET READY.

Recognizing that your future is in God gives you holy
hope, determination, and confidence. When you allow
Him to pull you into a life that is energetic, wise, and
wholesome, all worldly troubles fade and you are re-
made! Get ready. Jesus is coming. Live in a way that's
pleasing to Him.

*God, pull me into a life that is wholesome,
energetic, wise, and pleasing to You.*

DAY 165

Memory Verse of the Day

Now godliness with contentment is great gain.

1 Timothy 6:6 nkjv

WHAT IS CONTENTMENT?

To be content means you've settled an issue in your heart and you don't spend your days wishing and hoping for things you don't have. Longings and desires don't drive you to feel like you're somehow missing out on the "good life." God has already given you the best possible life through His Son.

Dear heavenly Father, thank You for the gift of a contented life through Jesus!

DAY 166

Memory Verse of the Day

"He will be great and will be called the Son of the Most High; and the Lord God will give Him the throne of His father David".

LUKE 1:32 NASB

JESUS CHANGED EVERYTHING.

Jesus changed everything. Think about that today. The little baby in the manger changed history, established the Church, and has changed your very life. Your family will never be the same. The world will never be the same. God's people will never be the same. . .and all because of Jesus.

Thank You, Jesus. Thank You for changing the world.

DAY 167

Memory Verse of the Day

"For the life of every living thing is in his hand,
and the breath of every human being."
JOB 12:10 NLT

I AM IN HIS HANDS.

Think about this: Is there a better place to be than in God's hands? With Him you can survive even the most horrendous circumstances. You are joined with Him at the very core of your being. His Spirit and yours work together to bring you through the difficulties in life.

Lord, You hold me gently because I am
small and vulnerable. Thank You for
keeping me safe in Your hands.

DAY 168

Memory Verse of the Day

*Angels are only servants—spirits sent to care
for people who will inherit salvation.*

HEBREWS 1:14 NLT

ANGELS WATCH OVER ME.

If God hasn't already provided you with all the help and
protection you'll ever need, He also sends His angels to
care for you. Though you can't see them, they are there,
a constant presence in your life, sent by the Father to
watch over you. Feel their presence today.

*Angels, Lord! Angels constantly watching
over me. What a wonderful gift!*

DAY 169

Memory Verse of the Day

I bless God every chance I get;
my lungs expand with his praise.

Psalm 34:1 msg

GOD LONGS TO HEAR MY PRAISE.

How can you develop a spirit of praise today? First,
amp up your prayer time. Then, throughout the day, find
new reasons to offer thanks to the Father: the refreshment of a hot shower, food to satisfy hunger, the smile
of a friend, the change of seasons. . .the list is endless!

Father, I praise You for this new day.
Open my eyes to endless reasons to thank You.

DAY 170

Memory Verse of the Day

Be still, and know that I am God: I will be exalted among the heathen, I will be exalted in the earth.

PSALM 46:10 KJV

THERE IS STRENGTH IN STILLNESS.

God is found in stillness. Here is another verse to re-member: "In returning and rest shall ye be saved; in quietness and in confidence shall be your strength" (Isaiah 30:15 KJV). God says stillness is good for you. It is how you come to know Him and gain your strength from Him.

Lord, I will find time to be still during my busy day. I trust that in stillness You will renew my strength.

DAY 171

Memory Verse of the Day

*Don't be misled—you cannot mock
the justice of God. You will always
harvest what you plant.*

<small>GALATIANS 6:7 NLT</small>

SEEDS OF THE SPIRIT.

One of God's spiritual laws is that you reap what you sow. Are you planting seeds of the Spirit—such as love, forgiveness, and mercy? Or seeds of the flesh—hate, unforgiveness, and apathy? Work in the Spirit and you will reap God's riches—now and forever! Sow good seeds today.

*Lord of the Harvest,
help me to sow the right seeds.*

DAY 172

Memory Verse of the Day

Just as water mirrors your face,
so your face mirrors your heart.

PROVERBS 27:19 MSG

LOOK IN THE MIRROR.

Have you looked at yourself in the mirror lately? If so, do you like what you see? If not, check for a deeper source. Ask God to help you look into your heart and mind and reflect upon what you see. Work on that inner beauty, and your outer self will become simply gorgeous!

Search my heart and mind, Lord.
Give me insight into my soul.

DAY 173

Memory Verse of the Day

*Whoever conceals their sins does
not prosper, but the one who confesses
and renounces them finds mercy.*

PROVERBS 28:13 NIV

GOD IS MERCIFUL.

Sometimes we "sneak" a sinful action into our routine
when we think no one is looking. But God is always
looking, and our transgressions break His heart. Confessing our sin to Him isn't easy. Still, it's the only way
to receive His mercy. Be careful about sin today. It can
be sneaky.

*Father God, sometimes I allow sin
into my life. Please have mercy on me.*

DAY 174

Memory Verse of the Day

"Therefore, my friends, I want you to know that through Jesus the forgiveness of sins is proclaimed to you."

ACTS 13:38 NIV

HE WASHES AWAY MY SINS.

Have you ever seen a waterfall rushing over rocks, plummeting to the stream below? Then you have a good analogy of the "washing away" of sins. When you come to God with a repentant heart, He takes your sins and throws them into the water. Into the racing stream they go, never to be seen again.

Thank You for washing away my sins, Lord—washing them away forever.

DAY 175

Memory Verse of the Day

Immediately he spoke to them and said,
"Take courage! It is I. Don't be afraid."

MARK 6:50 NIV

HE'S HERE!

Learning to recognize Jesus' presence helps you trust Him and have the assurance that you can accomplish what He asks. You come to know His ways and sense His guidance as you spend more time with Him. You discover that He wants to walk beside you every day. Focus on His presence today.

Jesus, as You walk with me today, let me sense Your being. I know that You are right here with me.

DAY 176

Memory Verse of the Day

*If your gift is to encourage others,
be encouraging.*

Romans 12:8 NLT

I WILL BE AN ENCOURAGER.

You can be an encourager even if encouragement is
not your special gift. Encouragement flows from the
love of Christ living in you, giving you the power to
strengthen God's people. It doesn't take much: a smile,
some encouraging words, or simply your presence in a
time of need. Be an encourager today.

*Father, who in my life needs encouragement
today? Help me to meet their need.*

DAY 177

Memory Verse of the Day

He comforts us in all our troubles so that we can comfort others. When they are troubled, we will be able to give them the same comfort God has given us.

2 Corinthians 1:4 nlt

GOD, THE COMFORTER.

God is the greatest Source of comfort the human spirit will ever encounter. Think of those times when He has comforted you. Using that example, comfort others in His name. Who in your life could use some comfort today? Offer it in any small way that you are able.

Lord Jesus, sometimes it is difficult to know how to comfort someone. Guide me. Show me what to do or say.

DAY 178

Memory Verse of the Day

*The Lord God Almighty will be
with you, just as you say he is.*

Amos 5:14 niv

HE NEVER LEAVES ME.

When you have trouble feeling God's presence, you might ask, "Where are You, God?" Don't let the enemy tell you that God is not with you! God is near. Each day, tell yourself the truth: That He is always with you. Then He "will be with you, just as you say he is."

Almighty One, I will seek You today. Give me the sense of Your being all around me.

DAY 179

Memory Verse of the Day

Guard your heart above all else,
for it determines the course of your life.

PROVERBS 4:23 NLT

GET RID OF NEGATIVE THOUGHTS.

This morning, take an inventory of your thoughts. Are there more negative ones than positive ones? Imagine a broom sweeping away all the negative thoughts. Then replace them with the positive verses you have memorized. Those verses will freshen and beautify your newly cleaned "house" like a bouquet of flowers. That's heart smart!

Lord, help me to recall all the positive scriptures
I have memorized and to dwell on them today.

DAY 180

Memory Verse of the Day

*"Most assuredly, I say to you, he who hears
My word and believes in Him who sent Me has
everlasting life, and shall not come into judgment,
but has passed from death into life."*

JOHN 5:24 NKJV

FOREVER IS FOREVER!

Have you ever contemplated the word *forever*? It's the
kind of word that leaves your head spinning. Sure, you
can read those "happily ever after" books and wonder
about a limited view of forever, but God's version of
forever goes on, well—forever! Into eternity. Beyond
the limitations of your calendar. Think about it.

*Father, I hold tight to Your promise of eternity.
I can only imagine how wonderful it will be.*

DAY 181

Memory Verse of the Day

Command those who are rich in this present world not to be arrogant nor to put their hope in wealth, which is so uncertain, but to put their hope in God.

1 TIMOTHY 6:17 NIV

THINK ETERNALLY.

How much do you trust in worldly things? Remember that things are not forever. What you own represents much less than what God wants for you. Things don't have the power to change you. They only keep you tied to the physical world. So, today, get into the habit of thinking eternally.

Dear Lord, when I get too wrapped up in wanting some worldly thing, remind me to turn my thoughts toward You.

DAY 182

Memory Verse of the Day

The LORD's plans stand firm forever;
his intentions can never be shaken.

PSALM 33:11 NLT

GOD'S PLAN IS FIRM.

When your life seems to be crumbling all around you, remember that God's plan for you stands firm. He knows what you need and how to fix your brokenness, because His intentions toward you were formed before you were born. His plan is a better design than you could possibly invent for yourself.

Father, when my plans crumble, help me
to remember that Your plans for me
are better. They cannot be broken.

DAY 183

Memory Verse of the Day

If they obey and serve him, they will spend
the rest of their days in prosperity and
their years in contentment.

JOB 36:11 NIV

I WANT TO SERVE HIM.

Most of us love to be served. There's nothing wrong with being served, but the Bible makes it clear that listening to God's voice and then serving Him—with worship, kindness toward others, and so on—isn't just a good idea, it's a great idea! How will you serve Him today?

Lord, it's nice to be served, but today I want to
serve You by serving others. Show me how.

DAY 184

Memory Verse of the Day

Do not cast me from your presence or take your Holy Spirit from me. Restore to me the joy of your salvation and grant me a willing spirit, to sustain me.

PSALM 51:11–12 NIV

RESTORE MY JOY.

This world will do all it can to pull you down, to tell you to give up. When you're tempted to grow discouraged, remember that you stand in the presence of God, and that He has given you the gift of His Spirit for times such as these. Find joy in His company.

God, sometimes I feel overwhelmed and weary. Please restore my spirit. Help me to feel joyful again.

DAY 185

Memory Verse of the Day

My people will live in a peaceful habitation, and in secure dwellings and in undisturbed resting places.

Isaiah 32:18 NASB

GOD HONORS A HAPPY HOME.

God wants your home to be peaceful and happy, and that begins with you. Put a smile on your face and speak to your family in a soft, positive, encouraging voice. You set the tone of your home, and you control the pace within it. Make it a place of peace today.

Lord, guide me today to create a peaceful and happy atmosphere at home.

DAY 186

Memory Verse of the Day

If God is on our side, who can ever be against us?

ROMANS 8:31 TLB

GOD IS MY SUPERHERO.

There's no need to quiver and shake. You have the ultimate Superhero on your side! No one can harm you, for God is bigger, stronger, and mightier than any foe you may face. Simply shine the God-signal across the Gotham City of your mind. He'll be there in a flash!

How wonderful that with You in my life,
Lord, nothing can prevail against me!

DAY 187

They attacked me at a moment when I was in distress, but the LORD supported me. He led me to a place of safety; he rescued me because he delights in me.

PSALM 18:18–19 NLT

GOD IS ON STANDBY.

When you are at your lowest, you may be easy prey, open to attack by the enemy. But don't worry. God is on standby, ready to lift you up out of trouble and set you down in a safe place. Why? Because He loves you! When you are weak, He is your strength!

Lord, thank You for always being there.

Memory Verse of the Day

*You also, like living stones, are being built into
a spiritual house to be a holy priesthood,
offering spiritual sacrifices acceptable
to God through Jesus Christ.*

1 PETER 2:5 NIV

I AM A LIVING STONE.

Today's scripture makes it clear that believers are
"living" stones being built up into a spiritual house.
Think about that. You are a living stone. Not brick and
mortar—the stuff used to build an ordinary house.
You're alive in Jesus, and not just while you're on earth
either. You're alive for eternity.

*Thank You, Jesus, for giving me new life
and the promise of eternal life in heaven.*

DAY 189

Memory Verse of the Day

*Now it is God who makes both us and you
stand firm in Christ. He anointed us, set his seal
of ownership on us, and put his Spirit in our hearts
as a deposit, guaranteeing what is to come.*

2 Corinthians 1:21–22 niv

JESUS SEALED THE DEAL.

To be "sealed" means there's no chance of destruction after the fact. God's seal is perfect and indestructible forever. Think about that for a moment. When Jesus died on the cross, He "sealed the deal" for you. Nothing can "unseal" His eternal work on Calvary! He's even given you His Spirit as a pledge.

*Thank You, Jesus, for "sealing the deal"
on that "house" waiting for me in heaven.*

DAY 190

Memory Verse of the Day

"I looked for a man among them who would build up the wall and stand before me in the gap on behalf of the land so I would not have to destroy it, but I found none."

Ezekiel 22:30 niv 1984

I WILL PRAY FOR OTHERS.

When you ask others to pray for you, you're counting on them to help carry you through the tough times. Do you give the same consideration to those who ask you for prayer? Remember, they are trusting you to stand in the gap for them during their difficult times. Who needs your prayers today?

Father God, forgive me for not praying for everyone who asks me for prayer. I will try to do better.

DAY 191

Memory Verse of the Day

But they said. . ."You can't get in here!". . .
But David went right ahead and
captured the fortress of Zion.

2 SAMUEL 5:6–7 MSG

TUNNEL TO VICTORY.

David disregarded the naysayers, tunneled his way
into Jerusalem, and overtook the city! Follow his lead.
Today, ignore the negative voices, keep alert for other
choices, and if the wall before you seems impregnable,
keep searching for your God-given path. Your heavenly
Father will guide you to tunnel your way to victory.

I need a plan, Lord. Show me the way to victory.

DAY 192

Memory Verse of the Day

Go to work in the morning and stick to it until evening without watching the clock. You never know from moment to moment how your work will turn out in the end.

ECCLESIASTES 11:6 MSG

I WILL STAY IN THE ZONE.

No matter what task you undertake today, get yourself into the zone. Resolve not to give in to thoughts like, *What if this doesn't work out?* or, *How am I ever going to manage this?* Close your eyes, say a prayer, and let the Holy Spirit take control of your heart, hands, feet, and mind.

I don't know what today holds for me,
Father, but I trust You.

DAY 193

Memory Verse of the Day

Let the peace of Christ rule in your hearts,
since as members of one body you were
called to peace. And be thankful.

COLOSSIANS 3:15 NIV

PEACE RULES!

What does it mean to allow peace to "rule" your heart? In order for that to happen, you have to submit yourself to the process. You have to trust God completely, willingly approach Him, and say, "Father, I can't live in chaos and turmoil anymore."

Will you do that today?

Father, I give up. Please replace all the stress
in my heart with Your perfect peace.

DAY 194

Memory Verse of the Day

Accept one another, then, just as Christ
accepted you, in order to bring praise to God.

ROMANS 15:7 NIV

GOD WON'T REJECT ME.

To be accepted means you don't have to work to earn
God's love. There's nothing you can do to be "un-
accepted" either. God won't reject you if you make
mistakes. This is why God is so keen on us accepting
one another (fellow believers) in love. No judging. No
divisions. Just acceptance.

Dear Lord, thank You for accepting me,
just the way I am, all the time. I love You!

DAY 195

Memory Verse of the Day

As a father has compassion on his children, so the
Lord has compassion on those who fear him.

PSALM 103:13 NIV

MY GOD IS COMPASSIONATE.

How do you need God to show you His compassion
today? Do you need guidance for a decision? Ask Him.
He will show you what to do. Do you want someone to
talk to? He is always available. Whatever you need
today—forgiveness, help, wisdom—seek your compassionate Father. He loves you.

Father God, I'm so grateful for the blessing of
Your eternal compassion. You meet my every need.

DAY 196

Memory Verse of the Day

Cast your burden upon the LORD and He will sustain you; He will never allow the righteous to be shaken.

PSALM 55:22 NASB

I WILL GIVE HIM MY BURDENS.

Do you always remember to take your burdens to the One who can do something about them? We are called to release our cares to our heavenly Father. A cause with an effect is implied in Psalm 55:22: If you cast your burden on Him, then He will sustain you. Think about it.

Father, I can't bear my burdens alone any longer. In my weakness, You are strong. Thank You for Your promise to sustain me.

DAY 197

Memory Verse of the Day

The Lord your God is in the midst of you. . . !
He will rejoice over you with joy. . .and
in His love He will be silent and make no
mention [of past sins, or even recall them].
ZEPHANIAH 3:17 AMPC

GOLDEN SILENCE.

Remember this: God is watching you and knows every
decision you make. But no matter what you do, He,
unlike fellow humans, will never say, "I told you so!"
Instead, He will rejoice over you and love you! How
great He is! His silence about past sins is truly golden.

Thank You, God, for being silent about those sins I
have confessed to You. Your forgiveness is forever.

DAY 198

Memory Verse of the Day

*Though there are no sheep in the pen and no
cattle in the stalls, yet I will rejoice in the LORD.*

HABAKKUK 3:17–18 NIV

HE IS WHY I AM HAPPY.

Okay. So maybe things didn't go as you planned. Instead of wallowing in self-pity or fuming in frustration, praise the Lord for what has gone right in your life. Before you know it, you will have your focus where it belongs—on Him—and find your faith lifting you higher and higher.

I lift my voice and rejoice in You, Lord!

DAY 199

Memory Verse of the Day

He replied, "Because you have so little faith. Truly I tell you, if you have faith as small as a mustard seed, you can say to this mountain, 'Move from here to there,' and it will move. Nothing will be impossible for you."

MATTHEW 17:20 NIV

HAVE A LITTLE FAITH!

Today's verse teaches that a tiny amount of faith is enough. Think of it as a seed, a starting point. You don't have to wait around until your faith grows. You can put it into action right now. So, what are you waiting for? Plant a little faith today, and watch it grow!

Almighty God, I have faith, if only just a little. Help me to act on my faith today and trust You.

DAY 200

The LORD gives strength to his people;
the LORD blesses his people with peace.

PSALM 29:11 NCV

GOD-BREATHED STRENGTH.

God-breathed strength is the sort that invigorates you even on days when you feel you can't put one foot in front of the other. It's an inside-out strength. Do you need some God-breathed strength today? If so, acknowledge your need to your heavenly Father. Admitting your weakness is nothing to be ashamed of.

Father, I am so weak, and You are so strong.
Give me the strength I need today.

DAY 201

Memory Verse of the Day

You were bought at a price.

1 Corinthians 6:20 niv

I AM A PERFECT FIT.

When it seems others do not want you on their team or you find you're having a hard time fitting in, remember that you are part of God's family. He created you and formed you to be a perfect fit. No matter where you've been or what you've done, God has accepted you.

When I'm tempted to feel rejected or unwanted,
remind me that I don't have to look far to
find my perfect place in You.

DAY 202

Memory Verse of the Day

He restoreth my soul: he leadeth me in the
paths of righteousness for his name's sake.

PSALM 23:3 KJV

HE RESTORES MY SOUL.

Feeling down today? Turn your thoughts and prayers
toward God. Focus on a hymn or a praise song and
play it in your mind. Praise chases away the doldrums.
Thankfulness to the Father can turn your plastic smiles
into real ones, and as the psalm states, your soul will
be restored.

Father, I'm down in the dumps today.
You are my unending Source of strength.
Gather me in Your arms for always.

DAY 203

Memory Verse of the Day

*Little children, let us not love in word
or talk but in deed and in truth.*

1 John 3:18 esv

LOVE IN ACTION.

God doesn't just want you to read or talk about living a
godly life. He wants you to get out there and live it. You
can't grow a garden unless you get up and start sowing
some seeds. So stop talking and start walking! Change
your world with love in action.

Give me the courage to live Your Word, Jesus.

DAY 204

Memory Verse of the Day

His divine power has given us everything we need
for life and godliness through our knowledge of him
who called us by his own glory and goodness.

2 PETER 1:3 NIV 1984

JESUS GIVES ME ALL I NEED.

Today's memory verse is a reminder that Jesus has given you all you need to live the life He has called you to live. Reading the Word, gaining godly knowledge, feeds that divine power within you. Continue to learn of Him, and you will grow closer than you ever dared dream!

Lord, I want to learn more about You.
Lead me through Your Word!

DAY 205

Memory Verse of the Day

*I command you today to love the LORD
your God, to walk in obedience to him,
and to keep his commands, decrees and laws;
then you will live and increase, and the
LORD your God will bless you in the land
you are entering to possess.*

DEUTERONOMY 30:16 NIV

THE PROMISED LAND.

What "land" do you wish to possess? Perhaps you're longing for a lasting friendship or a new, working vehicle. Whatever you're waiting for, rest assured, God cares. He has blessed you to enter your "promised land," but the timing of that entrance is completely up to Him. Wait, and trust in Him.

Heavenly Father, help me to wait patiently for what I want. Please get my thoughts in line with Your will.

DAY 206

I sought the LORD, and He answered me,
and delivered me from all my fears.

PSALM 34:4 NASB

I WILL FACE MY FEARS.

Fear is the enemy's tool, and you can defeat it. How? By seeking God's help. Ask Him to help you be willing to acknowledge fear and bravely face it. This sounds easy, but when faced with crippling terror, it is harder than you thought it would be. Trust! God *will* help you. Believe it!

Dear Jesus, I know that You will help me to face my fears. I believe that, and I trust You.

DAY 207

Memory Verse of the Day

*You are all sons of God
through faith in Christ Jesus.*

GALATIANS 3:26 NIV 1984

I AM HIS CHILD.

As a Christian, you are a child of the King of kings, the Lord of lords, the sovereign God. He is the One who hung the stars in the sky, and yet He knows the number of hairs on your head. You are not just God's friend or distant relative. You are His child!

Thank You, Father, for adopting me through Christ as Your child. Teach me to live as a reflection of Your love.

DAY 208

Memory Verse of the Day

*That clinches it—help's coming, an answer's
on the way, everything's going to work out.*
Psalm 20:6 msg

GOD HAS THE PERFECT SOLUTION.

If you're going through a particularly stressful time, if
you need answers and they don't seem to be coming,
recommit yourself to trusting God. Don't try to figure
things out on your own. Instead, trust in the King of
kings, the Lord of lords, the One who created you. He
has the perfect solution.

*Father God, today I recommit myself to trusting—
not in myself or my own answers—but in You.*

DAY 209

Memory Verse of the Day

*"For the eyes of the LORD range throughout
the earth to strengthen those whose
hearts are fully committed to him."*

2 CHRONICLES 16:9 NIV

MY HEART IS COMMITTED TO HIM.

God is on a mission. He is constantly on the lookout for people who will perform His will. He's roaming the earth right now, and He's watching all your actions. Do a heart check. Is it fully committed to Him? If so, get ready! He's going to do a marvelous work through you!

I'm awaiting Your orders, Lord. Speak! Here I am!

DAY 210

Memory Verse of the Day

I will take care of you. I created you.
I will carry you and always keep you safe.

ISAIAH 46:4 CEV

GOD IS MY CAREGIVER.

Do you long for someone to care for you? God cares! He is with you from the time you were conceived to all the days beyond. God is your Caregiver, familiar with every part of you. He will bear you up and surround you with His protection. Rejoice in His presence; feel His love!

I praise You, my Caregiver, my God.

DAY 211

Memory Verse of the Day

"Ask, and it will be given to you; seek, and you will find; knock, and it will be opened to you. For everyone who asks receives, and he who seeks finds, and to him who knocks it will be opened."

<small>MATTHEW 7:7–8 NKJV</small>

APPROACH HIM WITH BOLDNESS.

God wants you to approach Him boldly, and to come to His throne room with a childlike sense of expectation. That is why He tells you to ask. To seek. To knock. Instead of timidly approaching your heavenly Father, you need to come into His presence with childlike anticipation.

Dear God, thank You for being so open to my requests. I am never afraid to approach You with my heart's desires.

DAY 212

The name of the LORD is a strong fortress;
the godly run to him and are safe.

PROVERBS 18:10 NLT

JESUS IS MY SAFE PLACE.

Remember childhood games that involved a "base" (a safe place) you could run to? There is still a "base" that you can run to, one where you're completely and totally safe—from harm, from pain, from distress, from anything! That base is the Lord Jesus. Trust Him to keep you safe today.

Jesus, thank You for being my safe place to run to.
I know I am safe today, because You are with me.

DAY 213

Memory Verse of the Day

Now faith is being sure of what we hope for and certain of what we do not see.

HEBREWS 11:1 NIV 1984

WHAT I SEE IS NOT WHAT I GET!

What you see right now, how you feel, is not a picture of what your faith is producing. Your faith is active, and God is busy working to make all things come together and benefit you. In the same way, your faith works behind the scenes of your life to produce a God-inspired outcome to situations you face. What you see is not what you get when you walk by faith.

Heavenly Father, what I see today is not what I'm going to get. Thank You for working behind the scenes to bring about the very best for my life.

DAY 214

Memory Verse of the Day

So the cloud of the LORD was over the tabernacle by day, and fire was in the cloud by night, in the sight of all the house of Israel during all their travels.
EXODUS 40:38 NIV 1984

HE LIGHTS MY WAY.

Rest assured, God will shine His light on your travels, just as He led the Israelites with a cloud by day and a fire by night. Allow Him to lead you. His guidance will be accompanied with peace, joy, and a certainty that you have followed the One who has your best interests at heart.

Faithful Father, I praise You for Your compassion and concern for me. Go before me today. Lead me.

DAY 215

Memory Verse of the Day

Peter asked Jesus, "What about him, Lord?"
Jesus replied, "If I want him to remain alive until I
return, what is that to you? As for you, follow me."
JOHN 21:21–22 NLT

ON COURSE WITH THE SOURCE.

Remember this today: Jesus wants you to follow Him
and not stick your nose into assignments He's given
to others. If the urge to be a ministry meddler strikes,
turn your eyes back to Jesus before you trip up. Get
back on course with the Source. Follow Him full-force!

Jesus, I'm following right behind You—
You are my Source and my Guide.

DAY 216

*Depart from evil and do good; seek, inquire for,
and crave peace and pursue (go after) it!*
PSALM 34:14 AMPC

SWALLOW THOSE WORDS.

Have a word on the tip of your tongue, a word you're
dying to say but know will cause another person pain?
Eschew it, and swallow it down! Ask God for help.
He knows what's going on in your mind and in your
listener's heart. He'll supply you with the right words.

*Keep me from speaking and doing evil,
Lord. I want peace!*

DAY 217

Memory Verse of the Day

*For I am convinced that neither death,
nor life, nor angels, nor principalities,
nor things present, nor things to come,
nor powers, nor height, nor depth, nor any
other created thing, will be able to separate us
from the love of God, which is in Christ Jesus our Lord.*

ROMANS 8:38–39 NASB

GOD WILL NEVER LEAVE ME.

Have you ever been separated from someone you loved?
It's hard to be apart, isn't it? You go through a period of
grieving, for sure, and wonder if you'll see each other
again. This is only natural. What a blessed privilege to
know that you'll never be separated from God. Dwell
on that today.

*Father God, when I feel that pain
of separation, remind me that You are
with me, loving me and comforting me.*

DAY 218

Memory Verse of the Day

*Casting all your anxiety on Him,
because He cares for you.*

1 Peter 5:7 nasb

I WILL CAST MY CARES ON HIM.

When you fish, you know to cast your line into the water. It takes preparation, aim, and a sense of release. This is true when you cast your cares/anxieties on the Lord. It's a deliberate act: Make up your mind (prepare), place your worries at His feet (aim), and then let go (release)!

*Lord, teach me to prepare, aim, and release
my cares to You. I need to let them go.*

DAY 219

Memory Verse of the Day

*When I consider your heavens, the work
of your fingers, the moon and the stars,
which you have set in place, what is man,
that you are mindful of him, the son
of man that you care for him?*

PSALM 8:3–4 NIV 1984

HE CARES FOR ME.

When you ponder God's creation—the heavens, the moon, and the stars—do you feel tiny in comparison? You might be just a speck in the universe, but your heavenly Father says you are more important to Him than the sun, moon, and stars. He created you in His image, and He cares for you.

*Who am I, God, that You would think twice
about me? And yet You do. You love me,
and for that I'm eternally grateful!*

DAY 220

Memory Verse of the Day

You've kept track of my every toss and turn through the sleepless nights, each tear entered in your ledger, each ache written in your book.

Psalm 56:8 msg

HE COUNTS MY TEARS.

You live in a fallen world. There are heartaches and disappointments. Some cause you to weep at times. God hates to see you cry, but remember this: He knows the big picture. Good things are coming your way. Until then, allow God to comfort you and dry your tears. He loves you.

Father, remind me that You are a God who sees my pain. Comfort me in my times of sadness.

DAY 221

Lead a life worthy of your calling,
for you have been called by God.

Ephesians 4:1 NLT

EVERYONE HAS A PURPOSE.

Everyone has a calling—a God-given purpose. To live a worthy life, you need to follow the path where God is leading you. Give this some thought today: Where do your talents lie? Do you feel God urging you to use them for Him? This might be your calling.

Lord, I want to live a worthy life for You!
How can I use the talents You gave me?

DAY 222

Memory Verse of the Day

God did not give us a spirit of timidity, but a spirit of power, of love and of self-discipline.

2 Timothy 1:7 niv 1984

HE HELPS WHEN I FEEL AFRAID.

The Holy Spirit, also called the Helper, gives you all the resources you need to overcome fear. If you discipline your mind to trust Him, you will be unbeatable! Tap into His inexhaustible power whenever you need courage, and your banner of love for God will lift you above the fear of man.

Thank You, heavenly Father, for the Holy Spirit, my Helper. Lead me to trust Him whenever I feel afraid.

DAY 223

Memory Verse of the Day

"Give, and it will be given to you. A good measure, pressed down, shaken together and running over, will be poured into your lap. For with the measure you use, it will be measured to you."

LUKE 6:38 NIV

GIVE. . .GIVE. . .GIVE!

Are you a giver or a taker? Want to overcome a "taker" attitude? Give more! That's right. Give even more. Giving turns focus from self toward others. Before long, you see the plight of the person you're helping, and it puts your selfish desires in perspective. Be a giver today.

Dear God, show me different ways to give.
Open my eyes to the needs of others.

DAY 224

Memory Verse of the Day

As for God, his way is perfect: The LORD's word is flawless; he shields all who take refuge in him.

PSALM 18:30 NIV

GOD IS MY SHIELD.

Marching bravely in front of the enemy without a proper shield would be foolish. It's equally foolish to think that you can battle the enemy of your soul without being properly equipped. When you trust the Lord, He shields you from evil. Let Him be your shield today. He's ready and waiting.

Almighty and powerful God, be my shield.
Protect me from the enemy.

DAY 225

Memory Verse of the Day

The LORD is good to those whose hope is in him,
to the one who seeks him; it is good to wait
quietly for the salvation of the LORD.

LAMENTATIONS 3:25–26 NIV

HIS TIMETABLE, NOT MINE.

Patience is more than a virtue in today's wild and hyper-sonic world—it is an essential survival tool for a happy life. Scripture records that miracles unfold on God's timetable, not ours. How are you at waiting? Are you able to wait quietly and patiently for God to show up?

Dear Father, I'm not good at waiting patiently.
Help me learn to lean on You.

DAY 226

Memory Verse of the Day

And God said unto Moses, I AM THAT I AM:
and he said, Thus shalt thou say unto the
children of Israel, I AM hath sent me unto you.

EXODUS 3:14 KJV

GOD IS.

Are you plagued with regrets? Do you fret about the
future? God doesn't. It isn't in His character to regret or
fret. Although He existed in eternity past and will be in
eternity future, God is neither past nor future. His most
revered name is I AM. God is eternally *present*.

God, sometimes my thoughts slip to the past
and the future. Help me, please, to live
more in the present—with You!

DAY 227

Memory Verse of the Day

Jesus said to Peter. . ."You don't care about the things of God, but only about the things people think are important."

MATTHEW 16:23 NCV

A GOD'S-EYE POINT OF VIEW.

Give this a try today. As you evaluate situations, people, and circumstances, work to keep God's perspective in mind. Although you may not understand why something is happening, be assured that He's got everyone's best interests at heart. Try to see the world with a God's-eye point of view.

Jesus, help me to look at things through Your eyes.

DAY 228

Memory Verse of the Day

When [Peter] saw the strong wind and the waves, he was terrified and began to sink. "Save me, Lord!" he shouted.

<small>MATTHEW 14:30 NLT</small>

FIX YOUR EYES ON HIM.

By faith, you climb out of the boat. You begin walking on the water and everything's fine. But when you take your eyes off Jesus, your faith falters. You feel the wind, see the waves. Panic sets in! Before you know it, you're sinking. Trust Jesus! He'll save you today. That's how He works.

Help me to get my eyes back on You, Jesus.

DAY 229

Memory Verse of the Day

"Therefore, whoever takes the lowly position of this child is the greatest in the kingdom of heaven."

MATTHEW 18:4 NIV

GOD GETS THE GLORY.

Everything you are—everything you will ever be—is because of God's mercy and grace! Humility is pleasing to the Lord. He's not keen on hearing you brag about all your accomplishments. Sure, you've played a role in those things, but ultimately, the glory goes to Him. Be sure to give Him credit.

Forgive me, Lord, when I forget that
You are responsible for my successes.
The glory goes to You. Thank You.

DAY 230

Memory Verse of the Day

Give praise to the LORD, proclaim his name; make known among the nations what he has done. Sing to him, sing praise to him; tell of all his wonderful acts. Glory in his holy name; let the hearts of those who seek the LORD rejoice.

1 CHRONICLES 16:8–10 NIV

MY LIFE IS MY TESTIMONY.

Here's good news, straight from God's Word: When you live a praise-filled life, when you continually call on God's name, you can't help but let others know what He's doing in your life. You don't have to worry about "how" you tell them. Your very life—loaded with praise and thanksgiving—will be your testimony.

Lord, help me always to set a godly example for those around me. Allow them to see You through me.

DAY 231

Memory Verse of the Day

"Then your Father, who sees what is done in secret, will reward you."

Matthew 6:6 niv

I LIVE TWO LIVES.

Think about this today: You live two lives. Your visible life is lived before others. Your secret life is lived solely before the Lord. Are they consistent? Sometimes the motives behind one's actions are to impress others. The real heart is revealed by what is done in secret, when only the Lord is watching.

God, help me walk consistently in Your truth.
May what I do in secret bring glory to You.

DAY 232

"I will take away their stony, stubborn heart and give them a tender, responsive heart, so they will obey my decrees and regulations. Then they will truly be my people, and I will be their God."

 EZEKIEL 11:19–20 NLT

DUTY VERSUS LOVE.

We try to obey God's rules. We pray, go to church, and give money to ministries. But how much of our obedience is out of a sense of duty? Meditate on this: God wants you to obey Him, not because you're afraid He'll punish you if you don't, but because you love Him.

Help me to love You more, God,
and to obey You because I love You.

DAY 233

Memory Verse of the Day

"Everything is possible for him who believes."
Immediately the boy's father exclaimed,
"I do believe; help me overcome my unbelief!"
MARK 9:23–24 NIV1984

WHO NEEDS A FAITH BOOSTER?

Everyone needs a faith booster once in a while. When your faith is waning, you can cry out to God, and He'll give you the grace and power to erase your doubts and replace them with belief. Don't wait! Build up that belief! It leads to the successful working of miracles in your life.

Lord, I believe! Rid me of all doubt!

DAY 234

Memory Verse of the Day

But [the apostles] shook off the dust from their feet against them and went to Iconium.

ACTS 13:51 AMPC

SPIT IT OUT!

When a negative experience leaves a bad taste in your mouth, spit it out and move on. Don't let your mind linger on it or become obsessed with what should've happened. Just shake it off. New and better opportunities lie just around the corner. Trust the Lord to lead you.

Father, I am stuck thinking about that negative experience. Help me, please, to shake it off.

DAY 235

Memory Verse of the Day

Who satisfies your years with good things,
so that your youth is renewed like the eagle.

PSALM 103:5 NASB

HE MEETS MY EVERY NEED.

Young eagles go through many changes before reaching their full plumage. Through it all, God gives the eagle what it needs. The same is true with you, God's child. As you grow and develop in your faith, you go through changes. Some might seem difficult, but God knows what you need when you need it.

Father, from my youth through my old age,
You provide for me. You always know what I need.

DAY 236

Memory Verse of the Day

*He satisfies the thirsty and fills
the hungry with good things.*

Psalm 107:9 niv

GOD GETS IT!

God won't leave you hungry and thirsty. When you come to Him—your spiritual "belly" empty—He fills you. How? With His love, peace, and joy—His provision. You won't walk away from your God-encounter saying things like, "I wish God understood all of the things I need/want." He gets it, and He cares.

*Almighty God, fill me up with Your love,
peace, joy, and provision. I'm hungry for You!*

DAY 237

Memory Verse of the Day

"This is how much God loved the world:
He gave his Son, his one and only Son.
And this is why: so that no one need
be destroyed; by believing in him,
anyone can have a whole and lasting life."

JOHN 3:16 MSG

MEASURED IN SOULS.

God measures His wealth in souls, and that should be your focus too. God loved everyone—the world—so much that He sacrificed His own Son so that people might live forever in heaven. Be ready to share that idea with others. Someone needs to hear it today! Watch for an opportunity to share.

Which people in my life need to know You, Lord?
Lead me to them, so I can tell them about You.

DAY 238

Memory Verse of the Day

*I would have lost heart, unless I had
believed that I would see the goodness
of the LORD in the land of the living.*

PSALM 27:13 NKJV

GOD'S ETERNAL GOODNESS.

God's goodness isn't just for when we get to heaven.
He wants us to enjoy our lives here on earth. God cares
about the things that you care about. Look for the
good that He is doing in your life, and find joy in knowing
that your Friend deeply cares for you.

*Lord, thank You for being my Partner on my
life's journey. I'm grateful for all that You
do for me—and for the joy I find in living.*

DAY 239

Memory Verse of the Day

The LORD will be your confidence and will keep your foot from being caught.

PROVERBS 3:26 ESV

CAREFUL. DON'T SLIP!

Ah, that moment when the conversation is going well, and then you let your words slip—and you find yourself caught in a relationship disaster. Learn from it. Before you speak, mentally run your words by God. You can trust Him to keep any relationship-ruining words from spilling out of your mouth.

Dear God, stop me from speaking any relationship-ruining words today—and every day!

DAY 240

Memory Verse of the Day

"I am God and not a human. I'm The Holy
One and I'm here—in your very midst."

Hosea 11:9 msg

HE IS HERE!

God is not human. He will not carry a grudge. He is not
imperfect. He will not leave you. He is holy and He is
right here—in your midst! Just reach out and touch
Him. Talk to Him. Seek Him. Feel His presence. He is
with you this morning, right now!

You are with me wherever I go, Lord!
I praise Your name!

DAY 241

Memory Verse of the Day

Consult God's instruction and the testimony of warning. If anyone does not speak according to this word, they have no light of dawn.

Isaiah 8:20 NIV

I WILL RELY ON HIS WORD.

As you have memorized the scriptures in this book, have you thought about them—*really* thought about them? Have you held them in your heart and called them out when you've needed them? Today's verse reminds you always to consult God's Word for instruction. Rely on *His* Word, not yours.

God, Your instructions are perfect, and I know that I should always rely on them. Help me, please.

DAY 242

*Yes, my soul, find rest in God; my hope comes from
him. Truly he is my rock and my salvation;
he is my fortress, I will not be shaken.*

Psalm 62:5–6 niv

I WILL NOT BE SHAKEN.

Grab hold of the promise in today's verse. Truly believe
that life's shakings won't affect you from the inside out.
God is your Rock. That means He's the safest thing to
grab on to. He's your Fortress, and when you take hold
of His hand, you won't be shaken. What an amazing
promise!

*Father, You are my Rock and my Salvation, my Fortress
in times of trouble. Protect me. Hold my hand.*

DAY 243

Memory Verse of the Day

*"So you must change your hearts and lives!
Come back to God, and he will forgive your sins.
Then the Lord will send the time of rest."*

ACTS 3:19 NCV

U-TURN!

We all have moments when we realize we've been traveling in the wrong direction. Then we come face-to-face with God—through the person of His Son, Jesus—and we do a quick 180-degree turnaround. When we make that turn and repent, He forgives us. Repent today. Ask God to help you go the right way.

Lord, sometimes I mess up and let sin get the best of me. I'm sorry. I realize that I've made a mistake. Forgive me and set me back on the right path.

DAY 244

Memory Verse of the Day

*I will sing to the LORD,
for he has been good to me.*

PSALM 13:6 NIV1984

A FOUR-IN-ONE WORKOUT.

Sing to the Lord this morning! Singing is good for you in so many ways. Physically, it exercises your lungs and your heart. Emotionally, it lifts your spirits. It also benefits you mentally and spiritually. So don't be shy about singing a praise song. Belt out a tune. Give yourself a four-in-one workout!

*Father, I will sing praises to You
because You have been so good to me.*

DAY 245

Memory Verse of the Day

*"Lord, there is no one besides You to help
in the battle between the powerful
and those who have no strength."*

2 Chronicles 14:11 nasb

I CAN COUNT ON HIM.

Nothing is certain in life. Things can change in an instant. God is the one sure thing you can count on. Riches, people, and possessions may fail you, but God never will. Face life with assurance that when you are weak, He is your strength. He won't let you down. That's His promise.

Lord, You, and You alone, are the only One I can always count on. Great is Your faithfulness!

DAY 246

Memory Verse of the Day

For we are labourers together with God:
ye are God's husbandry, ye are God's building.

1 Corinthians 3:9 kjv

I WORK FOR THE LORD.

God allows you to work with Him to accomplish great things for His kingdom. He could have chosen angels or another method to fulfill His work that would have required less dealing with stubbornness and excuses, but God chose to use *you*—His human creation. Work well for Him today.

Great God, it is an honor to serve You. Help me
to remember it is You whom I work for.

DAY 247

Memory Verse of the Day

"Why do you look at the speck of sawdust in your brother's eye and pay no attention to the plank in your own eye?"

LUKE 6:41 NIV

DON'T JUDGE!

Think about this today: God tells us not to judge others. After all, He doesn't look at your outward appearance. He doesn't worry about your political affiliation or anything else in your life that is open to interpretation. He looks at the heart and judges you by whether you have a personal relationship with Him.

God, please forgive me for the times when I have judged others.

DAY 248

Memory Verse of the Day

For sin shall no longer be your master,
because you are not under the law, but under grace.

ROMANS 6:14 NIV

TRAPPED.

Sin traps you in a life you don't want. You wish for better things—freedom, peace, tranquility—but they seem elusive at best. The only "master" in your life should be the One you've submitted your heart to—Jesus! His grace and mercy are a lovely substitute for the sins of the past.

Jesus, be my safety net today.
Keep me from getting trapped by sin.

DAY 249

Memory Verse of the Day

*No temptation has overtaken you except
such as is common to man; but God is faithful,
who will not allow you to be tempted beyond what
you are able, but with the temptation will also make
the way of escape, that you may be able to bear it.*

1 Corinthians 10:13 nkjv

MORE THAN I CAN BEAR.

Do you feel like your burden is too heavy to bear? If so, today's memory verse should bring great comfort. God won't allow you to be tempted beyond what you can bear. Instead, He always provides a way out. He longs to see you walk in total freedom, above the temptations of this life.

*Father, please, enough! I'm so done with
my burden. Please provide me with a way out.*

DAY 250

*Jesus Christ is the same yesterday
and today and forever.*

Hebrews 13:8 niv

JESUS DOESN'T CHANGE.

Rest assured today that Jesus remains the same—
yesterday, today, and forever. Minute by minute, you
can look to Him for guidance, reassurance, and peace
of mind. You can rest in the fact that Jesus, your Rock, is
always there, waiting to strengthen you and meet your
every need. Trust Him!

*Thank You, Jesus, for being my Rock,
my Refuge, and my Rest.*

DAY 251

*For all have sinned, and come
short of the glory of God.*

Romans 3:23 KJV

CONFESS, RECEIVE, MOVE ON.

Sin is not a politically correct topic these days. Yet God talks about sin all throughout His Word. Satan loves to remind us of our sins to make us feel guilty. But God never intended for us to do that. Instead, God wants us to confess our sins, receive His forgiveness, and move on.

Lord, make me ever aware of Your grace and forgiveness, so that I may move on without guilt.

DAY 252

Memory Verse of the Day

Taking the five loaves and the two fish and looking up to heaven, [Jesus] gave thanks.

MARK 6:41 NIV

IT'S ABOUT WHAT I HAVE!

Jesus' disciples saw what they didn't have. But you know better! Look at what you *do* have and give it to Jesus. He'll bless and then multiply it! And in the end, you'll not only be satisfied but also find you have more than enough! You'll go from lack to plenty!

Jesus, I bring what I have and give it to You. Do with it what You will!

DAY 253

Memory Verse of the Day

He fixed his attention on them,
expecting to receive something from them.

ACTS 3:5 ESV

I WILL EXPECT GOD'S BLESSINGS.

Remember that faith and expectation go hand in hand. When you pray, firmly believing you will be receiving what you've asked for, miraculous things happen. Today, make an effort to fix your attention on the God of all creation, the Doer of the impossible, and expect to be blessed!

Lord, praying in Your name
releases power! I believe I'll receive!

DAY 254

Memory Verse of the Day

This is the confidence we have in approaching God: that if we ask anything according to his will, he hears us. And if we know that he hears us—whatever we ask—we know that we have what we asked of him.

1 John 5:14–15 niv

GOD HEARS ME.

Isn't it wonderful to know that God's hearing is impeccable? Not only does He hear your cries, He tunes in to your whispers. He even hears the silent cries of the heart—the ones you don't vocalize. Today, His ear is ever inclined toward you, waiting for your next breath, your next word.

Dear God, listen to my heart and my whispered prayers today. Give me what I need.

DAY 255

*He forgives all my sins and
heals all my diseases.*

Psalm 103:3 ncv

GOD STILL HEALS.

Along with forgiveness of sin, the Lord's goal is for us
to live at peace in this life. Sometimes we forget that
we can ask Him to heal our bodies, our minds, and our
hearts. Remember: God is still in the healing business.
He longs to see us walk in wholeness. Believe it!

*Lord, pain and suffering are all around;
still I believe that You love us and heal
our bodies, minds, and hearts.*

DAY 256

Memory Verse of the Day

"Bless my family; keep your eye on them always. You've already as much as said that you would, Master God! Oh, may your blessing be on my family permanently!"

2 Samuel 7:29 msg

HE WILL BLESS MY FAMILY.

Today, recommit yourself to trusting God with your family. Don't fret, and don't try to fix people. That's not your job, after all. And besides, God's keeping an eye on everyone. He's said it, and you can believe it. It's in His master plan to bless your family. . .permanently!

God, I confess I sometimes struggle where my family is concerned. I want to fix people. Remind me—that's Your job!

DAY 257

Memory Verse of the Day

*By his divine power, God has given us
everything we need for living a godly life.*

2 PETER 1:3 NLT

JUST SAY NO.

Stress can make you feel like a grape in a winepress, but
there's good news. God has given you everything you
need—but you must choose to use the wisdom He's
provided. Don't be afraid to say no when stress says you
can't add one more thing to your to-do list. Limit your
commitments today.

*Lord, help me to do what I can do, and I'll trust
You to do for me those things that I can't do.*

DAY 258

Memory Verse of the Day

The LORD will work out his plans for my life—
for your faithful love, O LORD, endures forever.

PSALM 138:8 NLT

GOD IS ON MY SIDE.

Today's memory verse is a reminder of God's faithful, forever love. When all seems lost, when goals seem unattainable, when you feel unloved, don't despair! God is working things out. After all, He loves you. So, take heart! You've got the Supreme Being on your side today—and forever!

Take my hand today, dear Lord. Walk by my side,
and allow me to feel Your enduring love.

DAY 259

Memory Verse of the Day

"I leave you peace; my peace I give you.
I do not give it to you as the world does.
So don't let your hearts be troubled or afraid."

JOHN 14:27 NCV

PEACE LIKE NO OTHER.

Memorize today's verse and repeat it to yourself, again and again. No wonder the angels were excited when Jesus was born. He came to give humankind peace like no other. All you have to do to obtain His peace is commune with God. With that peace upon you, fretting and fear will disappear!

Today, Lord, I will concentrate on the
peace You give me in all situations.

DAY 260

Memory Verse of the Day

"This Book of the Law shall not depart from your mouth, but you shall meditate on it day and night, so that you may be careful to do according to all that is written in it. For then you will make your way prosperous, and then you will have good success."

JOSHUA 1:8 ESV

THE SECRET TO SUCCESS.

Do you want to be successful? Then meditate on scripture and put it into action every day. Especially concentrate on God's rules and promises. Today's verse reminds you to be careful to *do* according to what is written in God's Word. Allow His scripture to guide you toward success today.

Dear God, help me to do according to Your instructions, being careful not to add to them with my own thoughts and words.

DAY 261

Memory Verse of the Day

Jesus replied, "Very truly I tell you, no one can see the kingdom of God unless they are born again."

JOHN 3:3 NIV

HOW TO BE BORN AGAIN.

Being born again is one of the simplest—but most profound—moves you can make. When you acknowledge your need for Christ, humble yourself, and cry out for forgiveness for your past sins, He grants not only mercy and grace, but a whole new life. A complete and total fresh start!

Father God, I need Jesus. Forgive me for my sins, and grant me a fresh, new life.

DAY 262

Memory Verse of the Day

"Be strong and courageous. Do not be afraid or terrified because of them, for the LORD your God goes with you; he will never leave you nor forsake you."

DEUTERONOMY 31:6 NIV

I HATE TESTS!

Have you ever failed a test? You're not expected to sail through every one. That's why they're called tests! There is only One who has never failed a test, and He's proven Himself faithful in every area. Jesus won't fail you. In fact, He can't fail, because He's perfect. Think about that today.

Jesus, tests make me anxious, but I know that You will give me strength and courage to get through them. You've got this!

DAY 263

Memory Verse of the Day

" They are not of the world,
even as I am not of the world."

<small>JOHN 17:16 NASB</small>

WORLDLY MESSAGES.

The world sends messages about how we should look and act. But believers in Christ are not of this world. We are in it, but not of it. We are visitors here, and heaven will be our eternal home. Today, do your best to avoid believing the things the world whispers to you.

Father, remind me today to tune out the world
as I tune in to what You have to say to me.

DAY 264

Memory Verse of the Day

*The Spirit and the bride say, "Come!" And let him
who hears say, "Come!" Whoever is thirsty,
let him come; and whoever wishes, let him
take the free gift of the water of life.*

REVELATION 22:17 NIV1984

JESUS—THE BEST GIFT.

Jesus gave His earthly life away without our asking Him
to or paying Him. Love led Him to give all He could to
draw some to Himself. He knew many would deny His
gift, yet Jesus still offered Himself freely. Do you know
someone who needs the best free gift in the world? Tell
them about Jesus!

*Jesus, I accept Your gift! Thank You for giving
away Your earthly life so I can have eternal life.*

DAY 265

Memory Verse of the Day

The Lord is a refuge for the oppressed,
a stronghold in times of trouble.

Psalm 9:9 niv

LORD, LIFT ME UP.

Today's news media seem to bear nothing but bad reports. It's enough to beat anyone down—unless they make a concerted effort to turn their thoughts, hearts, and souls toward God. Will you do that today? With Him, you are safe. Let the Lord lift you above the world's chaos.

Dear Lord, when the world's news gets
me down, I know that You will lift me up.

DAY 266

*" You will seek me and find me,
when you seek me with all your heart."*

Jeremiah 29:13 esv

GOD IS ALWAYS WITH ME.

Did you wake up feeling far from God? It isn't He who has moved; you have. He is never more than a heartbeat away. When you come near to Him, whole heart in hand, He will be near to you. Concentrate on Him all day today. Ask Him to fill you up with His presence.

*Almighty Father, forgive me for pulling away
from You. Fill me up with Your presence today.*

DAY 267

Memory Verse of the Day

To the praise of his glorious grace,
which he has freely given us in the One he loves.

EPHESIANS 1:6 NIV

GOD'S UNMERITED FAVOR.

When you love someone, you want to bless them. The same is true with God. He loves you so much that He wants to freely bestow His love, His grace, and His mercy on you, even when you don't deserve it. That's why it's called "grace," after all—it's God's unmerited favor.

Oh Lord, I praise You for the grace that comes through Your Son, Jesus. Your love overwhelms me!

DAY 268

Memory Verse of the Day

*"For the L*ORD *your God is a compassionate God; He will not fail you nor destroy you nor forget the covenant with your fathers which He swore to them."*

DEUTERONOMY 4:31 NASB

I PLEDGE. . .

Think about the word *covenant* in today's verse. What does it mean? A covenant is a binding agreement, a pledge. Think today about the covenant you have made with God. What have you pledged to Him? If you haven't kept your pledge, remember His compassion. If you ask, He will forgive you.

Dear God, forgive me for not keeping my promises, those things I have pledged to You. I will try to do better.

DAY 269

Memory Verse of the Day

The king's heart is a stream of water in the hand of the LORD; he turns it wherever he will.

PROVERBS 21:1 ESV

WHEN RELATIONSHIPS GET TOUGH.

Relationships can be difficult. Even when communication is good and both people are Christians, there is still conflict when two human beings have a long-term relationship. How do we get beyond competing desires that conflict with each other and harm our relationships? By putting them into "the hand of the Lord"!

Father, my relationship with _____ is not what it should be. Take us into Your hands and help us.

DAY 270

Memory Verse of the Day

GOD, are you avoiding me?
Where are you when I need you?

PSALM 10:1 MSG

MISSING IN ACTION.

If you're in a season when God seems to be missing in action, take time to listen more attentively. If you still can't hear His voice, remember there are times when He chooses to remain silent. Perhaps He's just waiting to see if you're going to act on what He's already taught you.

God, why are You so quiet lately?
Are You waiting for me to do something?

DAY 271

Memory Verse of the Day

*"When my life was fainting away,
I remembered the LORD, and my prayer
came to you, into your holy temple."*

JONAH 2:7 ESV

I WILL REMEMBER THE LORD.

Think about today's memory verse. What image do those words *fainting away* call up in your mind? Fainting away—the light turns to darkness, and you slip into unconsciousness. This is what happens when you forget the Lord. Remember Him, all the time, every day, so your life won't slip away.

*Father, I will remember and call on You,
morning, noon, and night—always!*

DAY 272

Memory Verse of the Day

"Only fear the LORD and serve him faithfully with all your heart. For consider what great things he has done for you."

1 SAMUEL 12:24 ESV

MIRACLES, BIG AND SMALL.

Today's verse tells you to consider the great things that God has done for you. He has filled your life with miracles, big and small. The first of those miracles is you! He made you and gave you life. Spend today meditating on what else God has done for you.

Oh Lord, I could never thank You enough for all You have done for me, but I will serve You—faithfully.

DAY 273

Memory Verse of the Day

Guard my words as your most precious possession. Write them down, and also keep them deep within your heart.

<small>PROVERBS 7:2–3 TLB</small>

GUARD HIS WORDS.

How important for you are the daily memory verses? Today's verse tells you to guard them as your most precious possession. Why? Because they help you resist temptation, make wise decisions, and discern God's will for you. They strengthen and comfort you. Memorize them. Then hold them close so they're ready when you need them.

Heavenly Father, I will memorize
Your words and guard them in my heart.

DAY 274

In peace I will lie down and sleep, for you alone,
Lord, make me dwell in safety.

PSALM 4:8 NIV

AH, SLEEP. . .

How well did you sleep last night? Were you so busy juggling your job, family, meals, dishes, and laundry, that you were wound up like a clock by the time you finally tumbled into bed? Keep your mind on God today. Slow down, and tonight He will bless you with sleep.

I will keep my mind on You today, Lord. Remind
me to slow down and not let stress get to me.

DAY 275

*When I awake, I will be satisfied
with seeing your likeness.*

PSALM 17:15 NIV

JESUS IS THERE.

Picture a boxer knocked out in the ring. Everything
is fuzzy. Then, breaking through the fog and haze, he
clamps his eyes on the Lord. Not on his opponent. Not
on the crowd, but on Jesus. Wow! That's like what we
go through when we've been badly hurt. Jesus is there
for us! Remember that today.

*Jesus, when I've been hurt, I will remember that
You are there for me. You always are there for me!*

DAY 276

Memory Verse of the Day

Whom have I in heaven but you? And earth has nothing I desire besides you. My flesh and my heart may fail, but God is the strength of my heart and my portion forever.

PSALM 73:25–26 NIV

GOD'S STRENGTH SHINES THROUGH.

In your weakness, God's strength shines through. His strength surpasses yours, even on your best day. It's the same strength that spoke the heavens and the earth into existence, and parted the Red Sea, and it's the same strength that made the journey up the hill to the cross. God is your strength today.

Lord, invigorate me all day with Your strength.

DAY 277

Memory Verse of the Day

Do not be wise in your own eyes; fear the LORD and shun evil. This will bring health to your body and nourishment to your bones.

PROVERBS 3:7–8 NIV

NOURISH ME, LORD!

Feeling run-down? Has your spiritual fervor left? Obeying and living by God's principles produces life and health. Just as you exercise to strengthen your body, you must use your spiritual muscles to attain the strength, peace, and prosperity you need and desire. Ask God to nourish you today.

Dear Lord, please help me out of my spiritual and physical rut. Nourish me today.

DAY 278

Memory Verse of the Day

By faith Abraham, when called to go to a place he would later receive as his inheritance, obeyed and went, even though he did not know where he was going.

<small>HEBREWS 11:8 NIV</small>

WHAT IS REAL FAITH?

Real faith is stepping out into the unknown, willing to go where God has called you even though you don't know where you're headed. The great thing about it is that when absolute faith moves people, God moves mountains. Do you feel God urging you to step out in faith today?

Father, help me to walk in absolute faith. I'm ready to go where You lead me.

DAY 279

Memory Verse of the Day

"Neither fear them nor fear their words. . . . Neither fear their words nor be dismayed at their presence."

EZEKIEL 2:6 NASB

OH, THOSE BULLIES!

We all have to deal with difficult people: those who make us bristle in their presence or who say things that wound our spirits. Fortunately, you have God's protection. When you abide in Christ's love, you need not fear the bullies. Be brave. Be bold. Believe. And all will be well.

Father, when someone lords themselves over me or acts like a bully, I won't be afraid— because Your love protects me.

DAY 280

Memory Verse of the Day

*Jesus replied, "What is impossible
with man is possible with God."*

LUKE 18:27 NIV

INSIDE INTELLIGENCE.

Turn a deaf ear to naysayers who tell you, "It can't be
done." You've got inside intelligence! Jesus has told you
that, with God, the impossible is possible! He'll equip
you to do whatever you set your mind to do. That's a
great mindset! So, get busy today and do the impossible!

I can do anything through You, Lord. Watch me go!

DAY 281

Memory Verse of the Day

"Surely there is a reward for the righteous;
Surely He is God who judges in the earth."

PSALM 58:11 NKJV

I'M SAVED TO DO GOOD WORKS.

You don't earn salvation by doing good works. On the other hand, you are saved to do good works. Your "acts of righteousness" (godly living) should come as naturally to you as breathing. If your heart is linked to Christ, you should long to please Him in all you do. Is your heart linked to His today?

Jesus, my heart is linked with Yours today.
I hope to please you with everything I do.

DAY 282

Memory Verse of the Day

"Therefore be merciful, just as your Father also is merciful."

Luke 6:36 NKJV

HE TEACHES ME ABOUT MERCY.

Ponder this: God teaches us to be merciful by example. He picks us up and dusts us off after every tumble. No pointing fingers. No "Shame on you!" He simply brushes us off, gives us a holy hug, and leaves us feeling convinced that we're still loved, no matter what.

Oh God, thank You for being such a gentle and loving Teacher. Thank You for showing me mercy.

DAY 283

*Beloved, I pray that you may prosper in all things
and be in health, just as your soul prospers.*

3 John 1:2 NKJV

I WILL PROSPER.

What does it mean to prosper? Acquiring lots of money? Simply having your needs met? If you look up the word *prosper*, you will see that the definition includes the word *success*. When you're successful, you're making progress, moving forward. Ask God to help you move toward success today. Trust that He will.

*Lord, help me to move forward
successfully. Help me to prosper.*

DAY 284

*Therefore, there is now no condemnation
for those who are in Christ Jesus.*

ROMANS 8:1 NIV

I AM SECURE IN JESUS.

Your security is rooted in Christ's unconditional love for you. It is not based upon your performance, but upon who He is. There is nothing that can separate you from His love, including poor choices or disobedience. Nothing can pluck you from His hand. Jesus is yours, and you are His.

*Dear Lord, my security comes in knowing You.
Thank You for Your enduring love!*

DAY 285

Memory Verse of the Day

*"This is my command—be strong and courageous!
Do not be afraid or discouraged. For the LORD
your God is with you wherever you go."*

Joshua 1:9 NLT

I CAN HELP CHANGE THE WORLD.

In the Bible, women from all professions and backgrounds were changed by grace, and then, with the Holy Spirit's help, they transformed the people around them. God wants to use you too in the same way. Does that thought scare you? Whatever He calls you to do, don't be afraid—He will equip you for the task.

*Lord, help me to be strong and courageous
as I follow wherever You lead.*

DAY 286
Memory Verse of the Day

*I will always love you; that's why I've been
so patient and kind. You are precious to me.*
JEREMIAH 31:3–4 CEV

I AM PRECIOUS TO HIM.

Speak today's memory verse out loud while imagining yourself saying it to your child. No matter how naughty your child is sometimes, you continue to love them because they are precious to you. That is exactly the way God feels about you. Even when you sin, You are His beloved, precious child.

*Lord, I sometimes wonder how You can love the sinful
me, but Your love is always there, and I revel in it!*

DAY 287

Memory Verse of the Day

They were just trying to intimidate us, imagining that they could discourage us and stop the work. So I continued the work with even greater determination.

NEHEMIAH 6:9 NLT

I WON'T BE DISCOURAGED.

Sometimes people will stand between you and your efforts to get the job done. The same thing happened to Nehemiah when he was building a wall around Jerusalem. But he prayed to God to strengthen his hands and turned all the discouraging chatter into his own determination. You can do it too!

Strengthen my hands, Lord. Turn my discouragement into determination.

DAY 288

"The L<small>ORD</small> doesn't need swords or spears to save his people. The L<small>ORD</small> always wins his battles, and he will help us defeat you."

1 S<small>AMUEL</small> 17:47 <small>CEV</small>

HE IS UNBEATABLE.

God, your amazing God, cannot be defeated. It's a spiritual law—the absolute truth! He is Master and Lord over everything and everyone. So the next time you face conflict, remember that God is unbeatable. And He's here to help you overcome any foes you face. Keep that in mind today!

Dear God, whenever I face an enemy,
I will look to You for help.

DAY 289

Memory Verse of the Day

*"Most assuredly, I say to you, he who
believes in Me, the works that I do he
will do also; and greater works than
these he will do, because I go to My Father."*

JOHN 14:12 NKJV

GREATER WORKS?

Today's verse may be a tough one to accept. You might
say, "What? I'm going to do greater works than Jesus?"
Seems almost blasphemous, doesn't it? Still, the Lord
might just use you to affect your world in a major way.
It could happen. Brace yourself, because this is one
promise that could leave you radically changed.

*Jesus, I believe everything You say. I will never be
greater than You, but I believe that You can use
me to do great, even unimaginable things.*

DAY 290

Memory Verse of the Day

It is for freedom that Christ has set us free.
Stand firm, then, and do not let yourselves
be burdened again by a yoke of slavery.

GALATIANS 5:1 NIV

FREEDOM!

How do you earn freedom? You don't! Christ earned it for you on the cross. All you have to do is accept Jesus as Savior of your life. Liberty begins in that moment and lasts forever. You are no longer burdened by sin. Praise Jesus! Celebrate your freedom today!

Too often, Jesus, I take for granted my freedom
from sin—earned by You on the cross.
Today and every day, I am grateful.

DAY 291

Memory Verse of the Day

But now, this is what the LORD says—
he who created you, O Jacob, he who formed you,
O Israel: "Fear not, for I have redeemed you;
I have summoned you by name; you are mine."

ISAIAH 43:1 NIV1984

HE KNOWS MY NAME.

Did you know that God knows your name? He created you. He knows you. He put together your personality and topped off His masterpiece by giving you all sorts of likes and dislikes, dreams and desires, passions and preferences. Celebrate today because you are His unique design, His child, His beloved one.

What a miracle, God, that among all the world's people,
You know me, inside and out. You call me by name!

DAY 292

Memory Verse of the Day

"But store up for yourselves treasures in heaven, where neither moth nor rust destroys, and where thieves do not break in or steal; for where your treasure is, there your heart will be also."

MATTHEW 6:20–21 NASB

HIS PRIORITIES, NOT MINE.

Each day, you make choices about the priorities in your life. The world sends messages about how you should spend your time; however, if you listen to the still, small voice of God, you will learn how to "store up treasures in heaven." Quiet yourself and listen to His priorities today.

Eternal God, remind me of the importance of spending time with You.

DAY 293

Memory Verse of the Day

*So we say with confidence, "The Lord is my helper;
I will not be afraid. What can man do to me?"*
HEBREWS 13:6 NIV1984

DO YOU NEED A HELPER?

What are you facing today? Do you need a helper? God
is the very best. Just knowing He's there will ease your
mind and invigorate you for the tasks you face. And if
you remember today's Bible verse, and other encouraging ones, they will boost your confidence and spur
you on.

*Lord, I'm so glad You stand nearby,
whispering words of encouragement.*

DAY 294

Memory Verse of the Day

In your strength I can crush an army;
with my God I can scale any wall.

PSALM 18:29 NLT

THE FORCE IS WITH ME.

God gives you power to crush any obstacle you face.
Think of it like scaling a high wall, one that you thought
you would never get over. When you need a boost, an
unseen force—God—fortifies your body, mind, and
soul. By claiming today's promise, you can meet any
challenge you face.

I need a boost today, Lord. Give me
Your strength to get over the hurdles.

DAY 295

Memory Verse of the Day

*Whatever you ask for in prayer,
believe (trust and be confident) that it
is granted to you, and you will [get it].*

MARK 11:24 AMPC

BELIEVE AND RECEIVE.

God doesn't want you just to ask Him for things. He wants you to trust Him to provide, to have confidence that He will deliver. So the "formula" is to believe and then receive! The best thing is, the more you receive, the more you will believe. What an awesome paradox!

I believe, Jesus. I believe!

DAY 296

Memory Verse of the Day

*The Lord gives you rest from your sorrow,
and from your fear.*

Isaiah 14:3 nkjv

GOD'S PEACE.

Don't go through today feeling poorly. When sorrow, pain, and fear develop within you, the Lord will give you His peace. All you need to do is reach out to Him. He'll give you the touch you need. By focusing your mind, heart, and soul on Him, your problems will recede.

Lord, today I need the peace found only in You.

DAY 297

Memory Verse of the Day

*God never changes his mind about the people
he calls and the things he gives them.*

ROMANS 11:29 NCV

FOREVER GIFTS.

Think about this: You've just received a great present,
but after a while, it becomes ordinary and you use it less
and less. The gift-giver says, "Hey, if you're not going
to use that, I want it back." Aren't you glad God isn't like
that? When He gives you gifts (spiritual gifts/talents/
abilities), they are yours forever.

*Almighty God, thank You for all that You have
given me, and thank You that Your gifts are forever.*

DAY 298

Memory Verse of the Day

*A wise man is strong, yes, a man of
knowledge increases strength.*

PROVERBS 24:5 NKJV

JUST LIKE POPEYE!

Do you remember Popeye the Sailor Man? One can
of spinach, and. . .*bam!* His muscles pumped up, his
strength increased, and he acquired the courage he
needed to face his enemies. God's children get their
strength, not from spinach, but from the wisdom found
in His Word. So swallow a little wisdom today.

*Dear Lord, I want to grow in godly wisdom,
so speak to me through Your Word, the Bible.*

DAY 299

Memory Verse of the Day

In Him also we have obtained an inheritance, being predestined according to the purpose of Him who works all things according to the counsel of His will.

EPHESIANS 1:11 NKJV

GOD CHOSE ME.

Have you ever inherited something special? Maybe you received your grandfather's Bible or your dad's class ring. Such gifts are treasures. But as wonderful as they seem, you have an inheritance that is far greater—God's gift of eternal life. Think about it: He chose *you* even before the foundation of the world. Wow!

Thank You, Father, for Your gift of eternal life.
Thank You for wanting it for me.

DAY 300

Memory Verse of the Day

"Not even Solomon in all his splendor was dressed like one of these. If that is how God clothes the grass of the field, which is here today, and tomorrow is thrown into the fire, how much more will he clothe you, O you of little faith!"

LUKE 12:27–28 NIV 1984

HE LOVES ME MORE!

If God makes flowers, each type unique and beautiful, and if He sends rain and sun to meet their needs, won't He care for you too? He made you. What the Father makes, He loves. And that which He loves, He cares for. You are dearer to God than any of His other creations.

Lord, how wonderful it is that I am more special to You than any of Your other creations!

DAY 301

Memory Verse of the Day

*But do not forget this one thing,
dear friends: With the Lord a day
is like a thousand years, and a
thousand years are like a day.*

2 PETER 3:8 NIV

THROUGH GOD'S EYES.

Today's memory verse is all about time and patience.
Ponder it: "*With the Lord a day is like a thousand years,
and a thousand years are like a day.*" If you often become
discouraged with waiting, 2 Peter 3:8 gives you
a fresh perspective. It helps you to see your life through
God's eyes.

*Heavenly Father, patience is hard for me
sometimes, so make it easier by helping
me to understand "heaven's time."*

DAY 302

Memory Verse of the Day

*Every man's work shall be made manifest:
for the day shall declare it, because it shall
be revealed by fire; and the fire shall try
every man's work of what sort it is.*

1 CORINTHIANS 3:13 KJV

GET INVOLVED!

Do you genuinely wish to help bring glory to God?
If you get involved in an act of service, you will be
blessed beyond measure. We are all called to be useful
for Christ. When we do so willingly and with a servant's
heart, the joy that fills us will be indescribable and
lasting.

*Jesus, open my eyes today to those
with a servant's heart. I want to learn
from them how to be useful for You.*

DAY 303

Memory Verse of the Day

*This is the day which the LORD hath made;
we will rejoice and be glad in it.*

PSALM 118:24 KJV

GOOD MORNING!

It's a new day! A new opportunity to build on yester-day's endeavors or to make a totally brand-new start. So get your morning off on the right foot. Rejoice! Be glad! Go forth with a smile on your face, a praise song on your lips, and joy in your heart!

Lord, thank You for this marvelous day!

DAY 304

Memory Verse of the Day

Forget what happened long ago!
Don't think about the past.

Isaiah 43:18 cev

LOOK TO THE FUTURE.

When you keep looking behind you, at mistakes and hurts that occurred in your past, you're bound to trip up in the present. God wants you to keep your eyes open, looking to the future. He is going to do a new thing. You might even get a few hints from Him today.

God, help me to let go of the past
and focus on the future.

DAY 305

Memory Verse of the Day

He arose and rebuked the wind and said to the sea,
Hush now! Be still (muzzled)! And. . .there was
[immediately] a great calm (a perfect peacefulness).

MARK 4:39 AMPC

JESUS, I NEED YOU!

Do you think that Jesus is sleeping on the job? He isn't!
Jesus is always ready to calm any storm that comes into
your life. Have you cried out to Him lately? If not, do so!
Get down on your knees and shout for help. Before long,
the storm will fade away, and you will be calm.

The storm is too much for me, Lord! HELP!

DAY 306

Memory Verse of the Day

For he has rescued us from the dominion of darkness and brought us into the kingdom of the Son he loves, in whom we have redemption, the forgiveness of sins.

COLOSSIANS 1:13–14 NIV

OUT OF THE DARKNESS.

God will rescue you from your darkest days. Imagine wandering in pitch darkness knowing your enemy lurks there. Then, a shaft of light breaks through, sending the enemy running. You are lifted—physically, spiritually, and emotionally—to a place surrounded by warm "Sonlight" on every side. That's what it's like when God rescues you.

Dear God, whenever darkness covers me and I feel afraid, I know that You will rescue me.

DAY 307

Memory Verse of the Day

"They will fight against you but will not overcome you, for I am with you and will rescue you," declares the LORD.

JEREMIAH 1:19 NIV ·

GOD IS BIGGER.

Remember when you were a kid, how someone's size could intimidate you? A bully seemed meaner because he was bigger than the other guys. And if he had an older/bigger brother, look out! Here's good news: No one can outsize God! He's bigger than any foe you could possibly face, so you have nothing to fear.

Father, Your greatness, Your bigness, protects me from evil. My trust is in You.

DAY 308

Memory Verse of the Day

*Let the wicked forsake his way, and the
unrighteous man his thoughts; let him return
to the LORD, and He will have mercy on him;
and to our God, for He will abundantly pardon.*

ISAIAH 55:7 NKJV

GUILTY AS CHARGED.

Imagine that you are accused of a crime you're guilty of.
But the judge declares you innocent, ready to pardon you,
no questions asked. You can go free. You are blessed to
receive a second chance. This is what God does for you
every time you ask for His forgiveness. Think about it!

*Oh God, I am so blessed by Your forgiveness
of my sins. Thank You for second. . .and
third. . .and fourth chances! I love You!*

DAY 309

Memory Verse of the Day

And the words of the Lᴏʀᴅ are flawless,
like silver purified in a crucible,
like gold refined seven times.

Pꜱᴀʟᴍ 12:6 ɴɪᴠ

GOD'S WORD IS FLAWLESS.

Perfection. It's a word we use lightly, but what does it really mean? For something to be "absolutely perfect" means that it is flawless. God is flawless, and so is His Word. Every verse you have memorized, every word of it, is flawless today and forever. Nothing on earth compares.

Lord, Your Word is perfect in every
way. As I read and learn scripture,
teach me so that I may serve You well.

DAY 310

Memory Verse of the Day

Take the sword of the Spirit,
which is the word of God.

EPHESIANS 6:17 NLT

HIS INSTRUCTIONS ARE CLEAR.

The Bible is filled with valuable information for your mission on earth. God's Word can set your mind at peace and hold you steady through life's storms. The truth found within its pages is your assurance that no matter what you face in this battle of life, God will bring you safely home.

I'm grateful, God, that Your instructions
for my earthly mission are clear,
trustworthy, and faultless. Thank You!

DAY 311

Memory Verse of the Day

*You are a letter from Christ. . . . This "letter"
is written not with pen and ink, but with the
Spirit of the living God. It is carved not on
tablets of stone, but on human hearts.*

2 Corinthians 3:3 nlt

I AM A LETTER FROM JESUS!

You might be the only Bible a person will ever read.
You are a letter from Christ! When you share your faith,
be more than a hasty email: Be a precious letter from
Jesus and take time to let others know how loved and
treasured they are by the Lord.

*Father, help me to make the people in my life
feel loved and cherished. Help me to remember
that I am a letter from You as I interact with others.*

DAY 312

Memory Verse of the Day

*Daniel answered and said: "Blessed be
the name of God forever and ever,
for wisdom and might are His."*

DANIEL 2:20 NKJV

I WON'T TAKE HIM FOR GRANTED.

Read about Daniel in the Bible, and you will discover
his many trials. He came close to death more than once,
but God always saved Him. And Daniel didn't take that
for granted! He reacted with worship and thankfulness.
Think about this today: How do you react when God
steps in and helps you?

*Make me thankful, Lord, for all the ways in
which You bless and care for me. I don't want
my life to become laden with ungratefulness.*

DAY 313

Memory Verse of the Day

*You are my hiding place; you will protect
me from trouble and surround me
with songs of deliverance.*

PSALM 32:7 NIV

HE IS MY HIDING PLACE.

Look around you and find a place to rest today. When
you have found it, then look to Jesus. He is your hiding
place, a haven, a quietness in the midst of a busy day.
Give the Lord your worries, your troubles, and your
questions. Give Him your praise and thanksgiving too!

*Jesus, be my Refuge today,
my hiding place, my place of rest.*

Memory Verse of the Day

*We are more than conquerors
through Him who loved us.*

Romans 8:37 NKJV

GOD'S LOVE CONQUERS.

No matter what happens today, you will not be defeated. Nothing can keep you from God's love. It will always be with you, pulling you up off the ground and into victory—today and every day! Look for His love today. It might come straight to your heart, or through someone else.

*I am amazed at Your unfailing love, Lord.
With You on my side, I will not be defeated!*

DAY 315

Memory Verse of the Day

*"May you be richly rewarded by the LORD. . .
under whose wings you have come to take refuge."*
RUTH 2:12 NIV

RUN TO HIM.

When you feel bruised, beaten, and battered by the world, run to the Lord. He will give you shelter under His wings, mend your wounds, and give you rest. As you abide in Him, you will find peace, comfort, and rewards uncountable. If things get tough today, run to Him.

*Lord, I run to You today. I thank
You for making me whole again!*

DAY 316

Memory Verse of the Day

God doesn't lose his temper.
He's powerful, but it's a patient power.

Nahum 1:3 msg

HE IS PATIENT WITH ME.

God gets angry sometimes, but He can control His temper. That's why humans are still here. How's your temper? Are you as just in your anger with others as God is in His anger with us? Perhaps it's time to stop fuming and start forgiving. Give that some thought this morning.

Dear God, please help me to keep my anger in check today. I want to be a peacemaker, not a fighter.

DAY 317

Memory Verse of the Day

*Be strong, alert, and courageous. . .and work!
For I am with you, says the Lord of hosts.*

HAGGAI 2:4 AMPC

THE GOOD OLD DAYS.

When times get tough, people start to look back to the good old days. But God doesn't want you to get stuck reminiscing or wondering what could've, should've, or would've been. He wants your mind and eyes looking ahead, scouting out new opportunities. What new opportunities lie ahead for you today?

*Help me to look forward, Lord, seeking the
new opportunities You've set before me.*

DAY 318

Memory Verse of the Day

She is clothed with strength and dignity,
and she laughs without fear of the future.

PROVERBS 31:25 NLT

I CAN LAUGH AT THE FUTURE.

God wants you to be assured of His care, to the point of your being able to laugh at the future. He's told you that nothing can harm you. So what is there to fear? Gird yourself with His strength. Take joy in the day. Have a good guffaw with God!

My heart is filled with joy and laughter,
for You are my God!

DAY 319

Memory Verse of the Day

*"I've said it, and I'll most certainly do it.
I've planned it, so it's as good as done."*

ISAIAH 46:11 MSG

HE DOES WHAT HE'S PROMISED.

How are you at keeping promises? Sometimes people
don't mean their promises. Or they mean them but
somehow don't come through. God isn't like that. What
He says, He'll do—you can be certain of it. So dig into
His promises. Go forth this morning with confidence
that they're as good as done!

*I trust You, Lord, like no other, knowing
You'll make good on Your promises to me!*

DAY 320

Memory Verse of the Day

*Our mouths were filled with laughter,
our tongues with songs of joy.*

PSALM 126:2 NIV

GOD LOVES GIGGLES.

From a small giggle that you keep to yourself to a great big belly laugh, laughter is a wonderful stress reliever and a blessing from God. How many times have you been in an awkward situation or a stressful position and laughter erupted to break the tension? Thank God for laughter today.

Heavenly Father, I love knowing that You like laughter. Thank You for every giggle and guffaw.

DAY 321

Memory Verse of the Day

*Moses' arms soon became so tired he
could no longer hold them up. So Aaron
and Hur found a stone for him to sit on.
Then they stood on each side of Moses, holding
up his hands. So his hands held steady until sunset.*

Exodus 17:12 NLT

A LITTLE HELP FROM MY FRIENDS.

Moses, following God's instructions, stood on a hill
holding up the staff of God. As long as he held it, arms
high, the Israelites were winning the battle against their
enemy. When Moses' arms became tired, his friends
Aaron and Hur rushed in to help. How might you help
a friend today?

*Dear God, today's memory verse is a good
reminder of the importance of friendship.
Help me to be a good friend today.*

DAY 322

" *Worship and serve him with your whole heart*
and a willing mind. For the LORD sees every
heart and knows every plan and thought.
If you seek him, you will find him."

1 CHRONICLES 28:9 NLT

I WILL WORSHIP AND SERVE HIM.

What is your idea of success? God's view of success
might be vastly different from yours. You will find true
success in earnestly seeking after Him and following
His commands. He asks that you give yourself to Him
in worship. So seek God today—worship and serve
Him willingly.

Dear Lord, teach me to seek after
You willingly, with sincere motives.

DAY 323

Memory Verse of the Day

The highway of the upright is to depart from evil;
he who keeps his way preserves his soul.

PROVERBS 16:17 NKJV

FOLLOW THE RIGHT ROAD.

Life is a journey. There is a right road, and there are also detours—sin that distracts you from the path God has laid for you. Trust God to guide you today! In prayer, reflection, and self-examination, He will show you any wrong turns you took and set you back on the right path.

Oh God, give me grace to repent when I
have strayed. Turn me back on the right path.

DAY 324

Memory Verse of the Day

Adam and his wife hid themselves from the presence of the LORD God amongst the trees of the garden. And the LORD God called unto Adam, and said unto him, Where art thou?

GENESIS 3:8–9 KJV

WHERE ARE YOU?

Throughout the Bible, God asks us questions, inviting us to dialogue with Him. The very first question God asked called Adam and Eve to self-awareness: "Where are you?" Of course God knew where they were. He wanted to make *them* aware. Think about it: Where are you in your relationship with God?

Father God, I long for a deeper relationship with You. Here I am!

DAY 325

Memory Verse of the Day

Jesus used many. . .stories and illustrations to teach the people as much as they could understand.

MARK 4:33 NLT

BIBLE STORIES.

The Bible is filled with true stories about people facing all kinds of situations. As you read about kings, queens, battles, and banquets, meditate on the stories just as you meditate on your daily memory verses. Remember—God often uses His stories in the Bible to teach you about your own life.

Lord, I'm guilty of skimming over some of the true stories in Your Word. Help me to focus on them and the messages You have for me within them.

DAY 326

Memory Verse of the Day

"Give your entire attention to what God is doing right now, and don't get worked up about what may or may not happen tomorrow. God will help you deal with whatever hard things come up when the time comes."

MATTHEW 6:34 MSG

WHAT ARE YOU WORRYING ABOUT?

Is worry zapping you of your energy? More than 85 percent of what you worry about will never happen. What a waste of power! So, instead of wringing your hands, retool and refuel by fixing your eyes on the present and what God is doing right now. Your energy will increase, hands down!

Energize me, Lord, and keep me focused on what You are doing right now!

DAY 327

Memory Verse of the Day

"Don't be afraid. Just stand still and watch the LORD rescue you today. The Egyptians you see today will never be seen again."

EXODUS 14:13 NLT

I WILL KEEP MY COOL!

The problems or people that plague you today will one day disappear from view. So keep your cool. Don't be afraid or give in to the fight-or-flight reflex. Rest assured that God is handling the situation for you. All you have to do is keep still and watch Him work today.

Lord, I know You are working in this situation. Thanks for taking it off my hands!

DAY 328

Memory Verse of the Day

"Stop doubting and believe."

JOHN 20:27 NIV

RECHARGE MY BELIEF!

Today's memory verse is short, but oh so important! God knows that doubting decreases your faith. Believing revs it up. Where are you on the "belief meter" today? Need to be recharged? Tap in to the conduit of faith by committing this simple verse to memory. Then stop doubting and believe!

Almighty God, help me to stop doubting
and to trust in You, even more!

DAY 329

Memory Verse of the Day

"Because of your faith, it will happen."
MATTHEW 9:29 NLT

FAITH BRINGS
DESIRES INTO REALITY.

Today's memory verse is another short but powerful one, another promise from God. Memorize it and ponder it. When your desires are in line with God's will, then your faith is what brings those desires into reality. Think about that today. Because of your faith—it *will* happen! Believe it!

Father God, set my desires in line with Your plans for me. Then give me faith to believe it will happen.

DAY 330

Memory Verse of the Day

*Jesus Christ is the same yesterday,
today, and forever.*

<small>Hebrews 13:8 nlt</small>

YESTERDAY, TODAY,
AND FOREVER.

Change is everywhere, and although change can be good, not knowing what the future holds can be unsettling. Where you live can change. Jobs can change. Relationships can change. But there is one relationship that will never change—your relationship with Jesus. He is the same yesterday, today, and forever!

Dear Jesus, I take comfort in knowing that while other things change in my life, You will remain the same.

DAY 331

Memory Verse of the Day

We do not want you to be ignorant about those who fall asleep, or to grieve like the rest of men, who have no hope.

1 THESSALONIANS 4:13 NIV1984

GRIEVE WITH HOPE.

Sometimes we get the impression that grieving or crying implies that we don't trust God, that we don't believe He has everything under control. However, in today's memory verse, Paul teaches on the subject of death and is clear: Grieve, but not without hope. Can you give a grieving friend hope today?

Thank You, Jesus, for understanding the pain of grief, and for loving us through it.

DAY 332

Memory Verse of the Day

Let no one look down on your youthfulness,
but rather in speech, conduct, love, faith and purity,
show yourself an example of those who believe.

1 TIMOTHY 4:12 NASB

I WILL BLESS THEM WITH WORDS.

God hears the conversations of His children. As you spend time with others and speak with one another, your Father wants your words to bless the lives of those who participate. He wants you to build others up with the words you use. So, get out there this morning and build someone up!

Jesus, please touch my lips and allow nothing
dishonorable to pass through them.

DAY 333

Memory Verse of the Day

When he saw the crowds, he had compassion on them because they were confused and helpless, like sheep without a shepherd.

MATTHEW 9:36 NLT

MEET THE GOOD SHEPHERD.

Reach out and introduce someone to the Good Shepherd today. Live your life before others with authenticity and humility. Allow others to see God's peace in times of trials, the Father's comfort in times of grief, the Savior's hope in times of uncertainty. Be real so you can point others to Christ.

Jesus, I will do my best to live in a way that allows others to see You through me.

DAY 334

Memory Verse of the Day

God is not a God of confusion
but a God of peace.

1 Corinthians 14:33 ncv

WORLDLY CLUTTER.

How are you feeling this morning? Is worldly chaos getting the best of you? Are you confused about what to do? When chaos and confusion rule your life, serenity goes out the door and stress moves in. Do yourself a favor. Rid your life of worldly clutter and watch the peace rain in!

Dear Jesus, please help me to put aside
worldly clutter and set my thoughts on You.

DAY 335

Memory Verse of the Day

"Do not worry about your life, what you will eat or drink; or about your body, what you will wear."

MATTHEW 6:25 NIV

WHAT SHOULD I. . . ?

What should I wear to the wedding? What should I make for dinner when company comes over? Do you drive yourself stressful with questions like those? Today's memory verse reminds you not to worry about such things. Keep it simple. Keep your eyes on God, and He will take care of the rest.

God, help me to keep my eyes on You.

DAY 336

Memory Verse of the Day

*Before daybreak the next morning, Jesus got up
and went out to an isolated place to pray.*

MARK 1:35 NLT

MY FIRST PRIORITY TODAY.

Jesus knew what to do to refuel. In the still hours of the morning, He went off by Himself to a secluded place to connect with His Father. Follow His example, and you'll find your energy and devotion increase tenfold! Make meeting with your heavenly Father your first priority today, and every day.

*Father God, I reach out for You
at the start of this new day.*

DAY 337

Memory Verse of the Day

*By day the L*ORD *directs his love, at night his song is with me—a prayer to the God of my life.*

PSALM 42:8 NIV

HE CONDUCTS MY LIFE.

Your life is like a symphony. There are some highs and some lows, and God is there directing it all. During the daytime—when most of the major decisions of life are made—He's there, leading you, guiding you. Keep your eyes on His baton, and let His love direct you today.

I don't want to carry the baton, Lord. Willingly, I relinquish it into Your hands. Direct me today.

DAY 338

Memory Verse of the Day

God, God, save me! I'm in over my head.

PSALM 69:1 MSG

CRY OUT TO GOD.

Are you in over your head today? If so, cry out to God.
You need Him this day, this hour, this moment! You
need the One who made you and knit you together in
your mother's womb. You need Him to save you—from
yourself. Cry out to Him now. He hears you.

*Dear God, come and save me. My burden
overwhelms me, and I'm in over my head.*

DAY 339

Memory Verse of the Day

*Jesus called the children to him and said,
"Let the little children come to me, and do
not hinder them, for the kingdom of
God belongs to such as these."*

LUKE 18:16 NIV

CHILDLIKE FAITH.

To enter the kingdom of God, one must receive Him
like a little child. What is childlike faith? It's an innocent, fearless faith. It's a kind of pure, unsoiled trust
that leaves no room for distrust or sarcasm. Childlike
faith doesn't have to be accompanied by a ton of Bible
knowledge. A simple "I believe Jesus is the Christ, the
Son of God" is all it requires.

*Jesus, I believe that You are God's Son and
that I am Your child. Take care of me today.
Teach me, guide me, and love me!*

DAY 340

Memory Verse of the Day

"In the desert you saw how the LORD your God carried you, like one carries a child. And he has brought you safely all the way to this place."

DEUTERONOMY 1:31 NCV

SAFELY HOME.

Are you wondering where God is in the midst of your trials? He's right there with you! Reflect on the way He delivered you from trouble in the past. Know that He loves you and that He will carry you out of trouble again and again and again, until you're safely home.

God, my arms are reaching out to You.
Pick me up and carry me safely home.

DAY 341

Memory Verse of the Day

"Observe what the Lord your God requires: Walk in his ways. . .so that you may prosper in all you do."

1 Kings 2:3 niv1984

DO WHAT GOD WANTS.

You don't have to be half-Vulcan like *Star Trek*'s Mr. Spock to know how to "live long and prosper." Just check out God's Word. It has the formula, and it's a simple one to remember: Do what God wants you to do—you'll not only expand God's Kingdom, but you'll flourish in the process!

Show me what You want me to do,
Lord. I'm ready to prosper!

DAY 342

Memory Verse of the Day

*Though a host encamp against me,
my heart will not fear; though war arise
against me, in spite of this I shall be confident.*

PSALM 27:3 NASB

FOCUS ON JESUS.

When an army of evil comes marching against you, surrounding you on every side, don't be afraid. Fear gives the enemy an edge, because your focus will be on it instead of God. Keep your Rescuer, Jesus, in focus. He'll lift you out of the fray and deal with the enemy too!

*Jesus, my Rescuer, lift me up and away
from evil. Protect me from my enemies.*

DAY 343

Memory Verse of the Day

Honor the LORD from your wealth and from the first of all your produce; so your barns will be filled with plenty and your vats will overflow with new wine.

PROVERBS 3:9–10 NASB

I WILL PUT GOD FIRST.

God is not a God of leftovers. He wants you to put Him first. One way to honor God is to give Him your "first-fruits," the best you have to offer. Remember: Everything you have comes from God. The Bible calls you to give back to the Lord one-tenth of all you earn.

Lord, remind me not to separate my finances from my faith.

DAY 344

Memory Verse of the Day

His wife's name was Abigail. And the woman
was intelligent and beautiful in appearance.

1 Samuel 25:3 nasb

WISE ABIGAIL.

God blessed Abigail with wisdom. In the Bible, her brains
are mentioned before her beauty. And how well she
used her brains! She stood before a furious king and his
army, calming them with just her words. Think about
Abigail today. Read about her in the Bible. What can
you learn from her?

Dear God, thank You for using the people in
the Bible to teach me about my own life.
Thank You for the gift of Your Word.

DAY 345

Memory Verse of the Day

For thus said the Lord GOD, the Holy One of Israel,
"In returning and rest you shall be saved;
in quietness and in trust shall be your strength."

ISAIAH 30:15 ESV

I DEPEND ON GOD.

What is your definition of *strength*? God's Word gives
His view of strength—rest, quietness, and trust. These
words all reflect a state of dependence. Strength comes
when you acknowledge your weakness and your need
for God, ending your self-reliance, and trusting Him for
your needs. Strength, at its core, is depending on God.

Father, remind me today that You are not
asking me to be strong, but to depend on You.

DAY 346

Memory Verse of the Day

*I am certain that God, who began the good
work within you, will continue his work
until it is finally finished.*

Philippians 1:6 nlt

I AM A PRICELESS WORK OF ART!

Although you may not be where you want to be, think,
today, about how far you've come. Consider that you
are God's work in progress. He is continually working
within you, carefully shaping you into the person He
wants you to be. You are His work of art, priceless and
one of a kind!

*Thank You, Creator, for shaping me into
Your unique work of art. I love You!*

DAY 347

Memory Verse of the Day

For my thoughts are not your thoughts,
neither are your ways my ways, saith the Lord.

Isaiah 55:8 kjv

GOD KNOWS BEST.

You may not understand everything that happens in your life, but God does. After all, He's the Supreme Being, the only God, and He knows so much more than any human ever will. It's unfathomable. Just rely on His good judgment. He has what's best for you in mind. Believe it!

Lord, I don't understand it all.
But thanks to You, I don't have to!

DAY 348

Memory Verse of the Day

Be my strong refuge, to which I may resort continually; you have given the commandment to save me, for You are my rock and my fortress.

PSALM 71:3 NKJV

HE IS MY CONSTANT REFUGE.

God isn't available to save you just once in a while. He's your Constant Refuge. Minute by minute, hour by hour, day by day, anytime you need Him, God is there. So run to Him. Hide in Him. Return to Him, again and again, to build up your strength.

Here I am, Lord. Thank You for always being here for me.

DAY 349

Memory Verse of the Day

*"Who knows? Maybe you were made
queen for just such a time as this."*

ESTHER 4:14 MSG

WHY AM I HERE?

To live in God's will is no easy task. At some point, you
wonder, *Why am I here? What does God want from me?*
Like Queen Esther was asked to consider in today's
verse, you need to examine your life and ponder the
thought: Maybe God brought you to this very place for
such a time as this.

*Father, please show me the
purpose for my day today.*

DAY 350

Memory Verse of the Day

"Love one another,
even as I have loved you."

JOHN 13:34 NASB

A PERFECT KIND OF LOVE.

You tell Jesus you love Him, and His response is, "I love you more." You cannot comprehend that kind of love, yet you are the recipient of it! He loves you, not because of anything you've done, but because of His goodness. Isn't it reassuring to know that God loves you with a perfect, limitless love?

Jesus, thank You for Your love for me.
I hope You know that I love You too!

DAY 351

Memory Verse of the Day

*"No eye has seen, no ear has heard,
no mind has conceived what God has
prepared for those who love him."*

1 CORINTHIANS 2:9 NIV 1984

THAT'S NOT WHAT I EXPECTED.

Maybe you doubt the direction you felt God urging you to pursue. Don't quit! Don't give up! Press on with your dream. Failure isn't failure until you quit. When it looks like it's over, stand strong. With God's assistance, there will be another way, a higher plan, or a better time to achieve your dream. Trust Him!

*God, thank You for putting dreams
in my heart. I refuse to quit.*

DAY 352

Memory Verse of the Day

*Make it your ambition to live quietly
and peacefully, and to mind your own
affairs and work with your hands.*

1 Thessalonians 4:11 amp

TAP INTO CHRIST'S PEACE.

Do you want a peaceful, quiet day? You can have one
by tapping into Christ's peace and minding your own
business. Keep your mouth shut when you know you
should, and your mind on your work, and before you
know it, others will want what you have and God's
kingdom will grow!

*Jesus, thank You for Your peace.
May it spread today like "Sonshine"!*

DAY 353

Memory Verse of the Day

I said to myself, "Relax and rest. GOD has showered you with blessings. Soul, you've been rescued from death; Eye, you've been rescued from tears; and you, Foot, were kept from stumbling."

PSALM 116:7 MSG

GOD CHAT.

Talking to yourself lately? That's okay—as long as you're feeding yourself positive, uplifting thoughts. When you assure yourself of God's blessings and heed His instructions to allow your mind, body, and soul to relax, it's like a healing balm. Keep up the God chat all day long. It does you good!

Thank You, Lord, for Your healing words.

DAY 354

Memory Verse of the Day

*You shall be a blessing. Fear not,
but let your hands be strong.*

ZECHARIAH 8:13 AMPC

I'M A BLESSING!

God thinks you are a blessing. That's a great compliment from the Almighty! Just be brave and keep up the good work. You are going to change this world for the better, and God won't let anything stand in your way. Now, get out there today and be someone's blessing!

*Thanks for the encouragement, Lord.
With You, I cannot fail!*

DAY 355

Memory Verse of the Day

*She thought, "If I just touch
his clothes, I will be healed."*

MARK 5:28 NIV

THE POWER OF A TOUCH.

Remember that you should never underestimate the power of a touch. In today's memory verse, the true power of a simple touch is beautifully portrayed. Think about this: A touch communicates not only affection, but also affirmation and sympathy. Today, you might encourage people—or comfort them—with a godly touch.

Lord, I turn to You when I need comfort. Let me also offer those around me the comfort of a loving touch.

DAY 356

Memory Verse of the Day

To fear the LORD is to hate evil; I hate pride and arrogance, evil behavior and perverse speech.

PROVERBS 8:13 NIV

FEAR GOD?

Why does the Bible say to "fear" God? In reality, to fear God is not the same as fearing a creepy-crawly spider inching up the living room wall. Instead, to fear God means we have a deep respect and reverence for Him. He is the Almighty, the Creator of the universe, and He deserves respect.

I kneel before Your throne with the deepest respect for You, my Lord and my King.

DAY 357

Memory Verse of the Day

It is vain for you to rise up early, to sit
up late, to eat the bread of sorrows:
for so he giveth his beloved sleep.

PSALM 127:2 KJV

SLEEP—GOD'S GIFT.

How did you sleep last night? Sleep is a gift from God.
He bestows it on you for your health. Think about this:
Ignoring sleep is faithlessness. Long nights of work,
play, or worry show that you don't trust God to provide
for your needs. He says, "Sleep, and I will take care of
the rest."

Thank You, Father, for giving me Your gift of sleep.

DAY 358

Memory Verse of the Day

"She has done what she could. . . . What this woman has done will also be spoken of in memory of her."

MARK 14:8–9 NASB

I WILL DO WHAT I CAN.

God does not require that you be perfect—you can't be! All He asks is that you do what you can. But before you jump in to be a doer or a fixer, ask God to guide you. Ask Him to lead you to do what you can in alignment with His will. Then, act!

Father God, sometimes I forget to seek Your guidance before I act. Help me to remember, please.

DAY 359

Memory Verse of the Day

*Though I have fallen, I will rise. Though I sit
in darkness, the LORD will be my light.*

MICAH 7:8 NIV

LIGHTER DAYS.

Do not give up during the dark days of your life. Keep
trusting that the Lord will raise you up after you fall. He
will turn your trials into blessings. Better and lighter
days lie ahead, so continue seeking His presence today,
knowing that He will make things right.

*Lead me out of the wilderness
and into Your light, O Lord.*

DAY 360

Memory Verse of the Day

O LORD, You are our Father; we are the clay, and You our Potter, and we all are the work of Your hand.

ISAIAH 64:8 AMP

GOD IS THE POTTER.

Hold tight to this thought today: God is constantly working on your spiritual shape, transforming you hour after hour, day after day, year after year. You are a work in progress. Make yourself pliable in His hands, and before you know it, you'll be a beautiful work of art!

Keep working on me, Lord.
Make me utterly beautiful in Your sight!

DAY 361

Memory Verse of the Day

*"Beware! Guard against every kind of greed.
Life is not measured by how much you own."*

Luke 12:15 nlt

JESUS IS MY EVERYTHING!

The Lord never meant for you to be satisfied with temporary treasures. Earthly possessions leave you empty, because hearts are fickle. Once we gain possession of one thing, our hearts yearn for something else. Remember this today: Lasting treasure can only be found in Jesus. Jesus is enough. Jesus is everything!

*Dear Jesus, You are my "enough."
You are my everything!*

DAY 362

Memory Verse of the Day

There is no fear in love. But perfect love drives out fear, because fear has to do with punishment. The one who fears is not made perfect in love.

1 John 4:18 niv

PERFECT LOVE.

Perfect love is like light. God's love for you is perfect. It is complete. The sacrifice of His Son to reconcile you to Himself is the ultimate act of His love. Jesus came to you in your sinfulness, loving you first, so that you could love Him. Feel His love! Let it shine!

Jesus, my Savior, fill me with Your love today. Let it shine through me so others see.

DAY 363

Memory Verse of the Day

"For truly, I say to you, until heaven and earth pass away, not an iota, not a dot, will pass from the Law until all is accomplished."

MATTHEW 5:18 ESV

PERFECT POWER.

Today's memory verse reminds you of the perfect power of God's Word—the Bible. It is God's Law for living, and Jesus said that every word of it is true and alive until that day when God brings our world and His heaven to His ultimate forever.

God, Your Word is the ultimate power and strength. It is my direct line to Your wisdom. Thank You!

DAY 364

Memory Verse of the Day

Now when Jesus came into the district of
Caesarea Philippi, He was asking His disciples,
"Who do people say that the Son of Man is?"

Matthew 16:13 nasb

EVERYONE IS WATCHING!

Just as people watched Jesus in His lifetime, people
are watching you today. What are people saying about
you? What do your actions tell them about you and
your relationship with God? Jesus' words and teach-
ings were powerful, but it was His actions that caused
others to stop and take notice. What will people see in
you today?

Lord, thank You for reminding me
that I represent You in everything I do.

DAY 365

Memory Verse of the Day

*You have heard me teach things that have
been confirmed by many reliable witnesses.
Now teach these truths to other trustworthy
people who will be able to pass them on to others.*

2 Timothy 2:2 nlt

I WILL TEACH HIS TRUTHS!

You've memorized 365 scripture verses! Each has taught
you a biblical truth and brought you closer to God. The
truths you've stored in your heart are your arsenal for
whatever trouble comes your way. But God isn't done
with you yet! He wants you to share these truths with
others.

*Lord, I will be Your disciple. Today,
and every day, I will live as a reflection of You.*

SCRIPTURE INDEX

GENESIS
3:8–9 . . . . Day 324

EXODUS
3:14 . . . . Day 226
14:13 . . . . Day 327
17:12 . . . . Day 321
40:38 . . . . Day 214

LEVITICUS
26:10 . . . . Day 156

NUMBERS
6:24–25 . . . . Day 134

DEUTERONOMY
1:31 . . . . Day 340
4:31 . . . . Day 268
7:9 . . . . Day 73
8:17–18 . . . . Day 97
12:28 . . . . Day 19
30:16 . . . . Day 205
31:6 . . . . Day 262
31:8 . . . . Day 131
33:27 . . . . Day 140

JOSHUA
1:8 . . . . Day 260
1:9 . . . . Day 1, Day 285
23:8 . . . . Day 124

RUTH
2:12 . . . . Day 315

1 SAMUEL
3:10 . . . . Day 56
12:24 . . . . Day 272
16:7 . . . . Day 93
17:47 . . . . Day 288
25:3 . . . . Day 344
30:6 . . . . Day 137

2 SAMUEL
5:6–7 . . . . Day 191
7:29 . . . . Day 256

1 KINGS
2:3 . . . . Day 341

1 CHRONICLES
16:8–10 . . . . Day 230
28:9 . . . . Day 322

28:20 . . . . Day 77

2 CHRONICLES
14:11 . . . . Day 245
16:9. . . . . Day 209

EZRA
10:4. . . . . Day 95

NEHEMIAH
6:9. . . . . Day 287

ESTHER
4:14. . . . . Day 349

JOB
8:22. . . . . Day 130
12:10 . . . . Day 167
36:11 . . . . Day 183
42:2. . . . . Day 59

PSALMS
4:8. . . . . Day 274
8:3–4 . . . . Day 219
9:9. . . . . Day 265
10:1. . . . . Day 270
10:16 . . . . Day 47
12:6. . . . . Day 309

13:6. . . . . Day 244
16:7. . . . . Day 106
17:6. . . . . Day 89
17:15 . . . . Day 275
18:18–19 . . . . . . Day 187
18:29 . . . . Day 294
18:30 . . . . Day 224
20:6. . . . . Day 208
23:3. . . . . Day 202
23:4. . . . . Day 100
25:15 . . . . Day 122
27:3. . . . . Day 342
27:5. . . . . Day 66
27:13 . . . . Day 238
27:14 . . . . Day 138
29:11 . . . . Day 200
32:7. . . . . Day 313
32:8. . . . . Day 48
33:11 . . . . Day 182
34:1. . . . . Day 169
34:4. . . . . Day 206
34:8. . . . . Day 36
34:14 . . . . Day 216
37:4. . . . . Day 158
37:40 . . . . Day 82
40:3. . . . . Day 92
42:5–6 . . . . Day 143
42:8. . . . . Day 337

44:15 . . . . Day 26
46:10 . . . . .Day 170
51:10 . . . . Day 76
51:11–12 . . . . . . .Day 184
55:17 . . . . Day 15
55:22 . . . . .Day 196
56:8. . . . . .Day 220
58:11 . . . . .Day 281
62:5. . . . . Day 44
62:5–6 . . . . .Day 242
69:1. . . . . .Day 338
71:3. . . . . .Day 348
73:25–26 . . . . . . .Day 276
84:11 . . . . Day 32
90:14 . . . . Day 51
96:1. . . . . Day 16
103:3 . . . . .Day 255
103:5 . . . . .Day 235
103:13. . . . . .Day 195
107:9 . . . . .Day 236
116:7 . . . . .Day 353
118:24. . . . . .Day 303
119:9 . . . . Day 69
119:71. . . . . .Day 152
121:5 . . . . Day 84
126:2 . . . . .Day 320
127:2 . . . . .Day 357
131:2 . . . . Day 4

138:8 . . . . .Day 258
139:13 . . . . Day 85
139:14. . . . . Day 12
145:18 . . . . Day 7

PROVERBS
2:6–8 . . . . Day 10
3:7–8 . . . . .Day 277
3:9–10 . . . . .Day 343
3:26. . . . . .Day 239
4:23. . . . . .Day 179
7:2–3 . . . . .Day 273
8:13. . . . . .Day 356
8:17. . . . . Day 25
8:23. . . . . Day 80
10:27 . . . . Day 62
12:25 . . . . .Day 139
16:3. . . . . .Day 151
16:17 . . . . .Day 323
16:20 . . . . Day 49
17:22 . . . . Day 8
18:10 . . . . .Day 212
18:21 . . . . Day 94
20:7. . . . . .Day 119
21:1. . . . . .Day 269
23:7. . . . . Day 6
24:5. . . . . .Day 298
27:9. . . . . Day 13

27:19 . . . . Day 172
28:13 . . . . Day 173
31:25 . . . . Day 318

ECCLESIASTES
3:1 . . . . Day 5
4:9 . . . . Day 52
11:6 . . . . Day 192

SONG OF SOLOMON
2:15 . . . . Day 161

ISAIAH
8:20 . . . . Day 241
14:3 . . . . Day 296
26:3 . . . . Day 117
30:15 . . . . Day 345
32:18 . . . . Day 185
40:31 . . . . Day 40
41:13 . . . . Day 115
43:1 . . . . Day 291
43:2 . . . . Day 127
43:18 . . . . Day 304
46:4 . . . . Day 210
46:11 . . . . Day 319
53:4 . . . . Day 78
54:10 . . . . Day 101
55:3 . . . . Day 14

55:7 . . . . Day 308
55:8 . . . . Day 347
64:8 . . . . Day 360

JEREMIAH
1:19 . . . . Day 307
29:11 . . . . Day 9
29:13 . . . . Day 266
31:3–4 . . . . Day 286
31:13 . . . . Day 43
33:3 . . . . Day 155

LAMENTATIONS
3:22–23 . . . . Day 144
3:25–26 . . . . Day 225
3:40 . . . . Day 68

EZEKIEL
2:6 . . . . Day 279
11:19–20 . . . . Day 232
22:30 . . . . Day 190

DANIEL
2:20 . . . . Day 312

HOSEA
8:7 . . . . Day 86
11:9 . . . . Day 240

JOEL
2:12–13........Day 145
3:10.............Day 23

AMOS
5:14............Day 178

JONAH
2:7.............Day 271

MICAH
7:8.............Day 359

NAHUM
1:3............Day 316
1:7.............Day 61

HABAKKUK
2:3............Day 154
3:17–18........Day 198
3:19.............Day 41

ZEPHANIAH
3:17............Day 197

HAGGAI
2:4............Day 317

ZECHARIAH
8:13............Day 354
9:16............Day 135

MALACHI
3:6.............Day 116

MATTHEW
4:19............Day 70
5:4.............Day 55
5:13............Day 64
5:18...........Day 363
6:6............Day 231
6:7............... Day 3
6:14...........Day 125
6:20–21........Day 292
6:25...........Day 335
6:33............Day 22
6:34...........Day 326
7:7.............Day 58
7:7–8 ....Day 211
9:29...........Day 329
9:36...........Day 333
10:8............Day 128
10:32 ....Day 35
11:28 ....Day 108
14:30 ....Day 228
16:13 ....Day 364

16:23 ....Day 227
17:20 ....Day 199
18:4.............Day 229
22:37–39 ....Day 133
23:12 ....Day 149
25:21 ....Day 105
26:53 ....Day 18

MARK
1:35.............Day 336
4:33.............Day 325
4:39.............Day 305
5:28.............Day 355
6:31.............. Day 34
6:41.............Day 252
6:50.............Day 175
9:23–24.........Day 233
11:23 .... Day 53
11:24 ....Day 295
14:8–9 ....Day 358

LUKE
1:32.............Day 166
5:16.............Day 114
6:31.............Day 148
6:36.............Day 282
6:38.............Day 223
6:41.............Day 247

8:11.............Day 112
10:41 .... Day 71
12:15 ....Day 361
12:27–28 ....Day 300
18:16 ....Day 339
18:27 ....Day 280

JOHN
1:12.............Day 109
3:3..............Day 261
3:16.............Day 237
3:17.............Day 157
5:24.............Day 180
7:38.............Day 147
10:2–3 .... Day 90
10:10 ....Day 107
13:34 ....Day 350
14:12 ....Day 289
14:16–17 .... Day 38
14:27 ....Day 259
15:16 .... Day 11
16:24 ....Day 121
16:33 ....Day 104
17:16 ....Day 263
20:27 ....Day 328
21:21–22 ....Day 215

ACTS

3:5............Day 253
3:19...........Day 243
13:38 ....Day 174
13:51 ....Day 234
17:28 ....Day 17

ROMANS

3:23............Day 251
4:20–21.........Day 129
6:14............Day 248
8:1.............Day 284
8:28............Day 65
8:31............Day 186
8:37............Day 314
8:38–39.........Day 217
8:39............Day 21
11:29 ....Day 297
12:8............Day 176
12:9–10.........Day 153
12:12 ....Day 50
12:21 ....Day 150
15:7............Day 194
15:13 ....Day 20

1 CORINTHIANS

1:9.............Day 63
2:9.............Day 351

3:9............Day 246
3:13...........Day 302
6:13...........Day 162
6:17...........Day 142
6:20...........Day 201
10:6...........Day 110
10:13 ....Day 249
14:33 ....Day 334

2 CORINTHIANS

1:4............Day 177
1:21–22.........Day 189
3:3.............Day 311
5:17...........Day 103
9:8.............Day 79

GALATIANS

3:26...........Day 207
5:1............Day 290
5:25...........Day 91
6:7............Day 171

EPHESIANS

1:5......Day 57, Day 141
1:6............Day 267
1:11...........Day 299
3:12...........Day 39
3:20...........Day 2

4:1 . . . . Day 221
4:29 . . . . Day 46
5:15–16 . . . . Day 123
6:10 . . . . Day 60
6:13 . . . . Day 118
6:17 . . . . Day 310

PHILIPPIANS
1:6 . . . . Day 346
2:13 . . . . Day 81
3:13 . . . . . . Day 33, Day 67
4:6 . . . . Day 160
4:11 . . . . Day 28
4:13 . . . . Day 83
4:19 . . . . . . Day 37, Day 99

COLOSSIANS
1:13–14 . . . . Day 306
2:10 . . . . Day 113
3:3 . . . . Day 45
3:11 . . . . Day 111
3:12 . . . . Day 159
3:15 . . . . Day 193
3:23 . . . . Day 87

1 THESSALONIANS
4:11 . . . . Day 352
4:13 . . . . Day 331

2 THESSALONIANS
1:11 . . . . Day 96
3:16 . . . . Day 163

1 TIMOTHY
4:12 . . . . Day 332
6:6 . . . . Day 165
6:17 . . . . Day 181

2 TIMOTHY
1:7 . . . . Day 222
1:11–12 . . . . Day 75
2:2 . . . . Day 365

HEBREWS
1:14 . . . . Day 168
4:12 . . . . Day 72
8:12 . . . . Day 120
11:1 . . . . Day 213
11:8 . . . . Day 278
12:1 . . . . Day 98
13:2 . . . . Day 54
13:6 . . . . Day 293
13:8 . . . Day 250, Day 330

JAMES
1:12 . . . . Day 74

1:17. . . . . Day 24
1:22. . . . . Day 42
5:16. . . . . Day 31

1 PETER
1:8. . . . . Day 88
1:13. . . . . .Day 164
2:5. . . . . .Day 188
3:3–4 . . . . .Day 102
4:10. . . . . Day 30
5:7. . . . . .Day 218

2 PETER
1:3. . . . Day 204, Day 257
1:4. . . . . .Day 132
3:8. . . . Day 146, Day 301

1 JOHN
1:7. . . . . .Day 136
2:6. . . . . Day 27
3:18. . . . . .Day 203
4:4. . . . . .Day 126
4:18. . . . . .Day 362
5:14–15. . . . . .Day 254

3 JOHN
1:2. . . . . .Day 283
1:11. . . . . Day 29

REVELATION
22:17 . . . . .Day 264

BIBLE ENCOURAGEMENT FOR YOUR HEART

60-Second Refreshment: Daily Messages from God's Heart

Open your heart to God's special message for you with the *60 Second Refreshment: Daily Messages from God's Heart*, filled with inspirational quotes, thoughts, and prayers to lighten your day and brighten your way!

Hardback / 978-1-63609-038-2 / $12.99

Nevertheless, She Was Chosen

Grow deeper in your faith as you grow ever closer to the heavenly Father, who loves you unconditionally. Dozens of practical and encouraging devotions inspired by 1 Peter 2:9–10 will draw you closer to His heart.

Hardback / 978-1-63609-092-4 / $14.99